Lizzie Scott has asserted her right to be identified as the author of this Work in accordance with the Copyright, Designs and Patents Act 1988

All rights reserved.

No part of this publication may be reproduced, stored in a retrieval system, or transmitted, in any form or by any means, electronic, mechanical, photocopying, recording or otherwise, without the prior permission in writing of the copyright owner, nor be otherwise circulated in any form of binding or cover other than that in which it is published and without a similar condition including this condition

This book is dedicated to my Darling Husband Howard, our children and extended family members who all gave so much for one very special little lady.

It is also dedicated to the memory of Mia

With thanks for all she taught me.

Heavens special child

A meeting was held quite far from earth
It's time again for another birth
Said the angels to the Lord above
This special child will need much love
Her progress may seem very slow
Accomplishments she may not show
And she will require extra care
From folks she meets way down there
She may not laugh or run or play
Her thoughts may seem quite far away
In many ways she won't adapt
And she will be known as handicapped
So let's be careful where she is sent
We want her life to be content
Please Lord, find the parent who
Will do a special job for you
They will not realise right away
The leading role they are asked to play
But with this child from above
Comes stronger Faith and richer Love
And soon they'll know the privilege given
In caring for this child from Heaven
This precious charge so meek and mild
Is Heavens "Very Special Child"

(Author unknown)

Chapter 1

"The answers no"

"Please Lorraine, think again..."

"Look Sarah," I said, "I've had this same discussion for the past week with team leaders; link workers; social workers... they all got the same answer. Now they get you to phone and add pressure to me. It's just not fair. I don't feel capable of doing this."

"And what's more... it's got to be written somewhere on our profile the sort of children we will take in"

We were not fussy foster carers, we just knew our comfort zone and liked to stay in it, though this wasn't always easy because sometimes; most times; we started off in our comfort zone then events somehow took us spiralling out of it.

We did not however, like to start outside of it and then spiral further away from what we knew we could do. Oh no; that could be disastrous for everyone involved, especially the child or children that had been placed with us.

"You can't just expect us to say yes all the time...sometimes you are just going to have to accept the no word...like now."

I don't care what you say...go down on your knees...the answer will not be different for you even though I do like and respect you.

Sarah had listened patiently to me as I rattled on about the unfairness of social workers putting pressure onto foster carers.

When we had started fostering years ago we were allowed to say no to all kinds of placements; no boys or perhaps you didn't want girls; no black children or you could turn away white children; no Catholics; Protestants; Jews; no disabilities... no; no; no.

You could be so picky it was untrue.

And at the risk of getting a slapped wrist...

It was fair.

How cruel is it to place a child with a family that really don't want them to be there, because they are the wrong colour or religion or even the wrong sex?

That must be torture for the child...to be removed from a birth family that is dysfunctional, only to be placed with a family that will 'tolerate' you.

That type of foster family is as dysfunctional, albeit on another level, as the birth family.

No; it is definitely much better to have some choice thrown into the equation.

All we had said no to was a child with disabilities.

By disability we meant major issues with mobility or severe mental disability. I didn't feel it was fair on our young family to take on a child that could be so demanding of our time, meaning normal days out became too difficult to manage; though know many people do manage and manage very well.

We were happy to work with children who had the smaller disabilities like poor hearing or poor eye sight even a minor learning disability would be manageable and still allow for each child to have some 'special' time just for themselves with us as their parents.

Know your capabilities I thought.

Not of course that anyone starting out on the rocky road of fostering can possibly know their capabilities.

They may think they do but, it's a funny road to travel as you come up to so many sign posts along the way.

None of them point to the easy route.

Now Howard and I had been happy to care for any child when we first started our fostering career.

Well...so long as they had two arms; two legs; a mouth that worked; and ears that heard.

Being quite naive we figured that just about covered everyone.

And anyway...even post training, initially we still thought we were only going to be looking after kids who had been hit too hard or not fed properly...

Had we known then what we learned on this new journey, maybe we should have said no children who have been sexually abused; under fed; over fed; no child who has had the shite beat out of him; hot baths; cold baths; no child who had druggies for parents...or alcoholics...

And yes, to the child who has disabilities...

But I digress; we started or fostering career like so many other's...

Blissfully unaware of exactly what we were getting our family into.

Okay...I'll settle for vocation because I suppose that was what it was.

Now it's a career where you can earn big money if you work for the right agency and, from what I've seen from some of the 'carers' I've met over the years, you don't even have to be that good.

Like birth parents...for some reason foster carers standards now have to be just 'good enough.'

Whatever 'Just good enough' means.

For Howard and I, knowing our capabilities and working within that framework, meant taking in who we felt we could care for in the same way we cared for our own children.

We had always given a service to the social services that we would want our children to have if they had ever been in the sad situation of needing to be fostered.

Hell would freeze over before I allowed any of my kids into some of the foster homes I've been in though.

God there are some skanky families out there...but they are nice people you see...

No, to be honest I didn't either.

I would eventually get so fed up with the 'non-judgmental political correctness' of it all.

So what if I judged people.

This was real life.

I don't think there is a person alive that doesn't pass judgement every day on someone...even if it's just to admire a pretty face or complain about a meal.

We are judging.

One social worker told me my standards were too high.

What a laugh.

I considered my standards to be normal.

Clean children... until they went out to play then they were dirty children... no problem because there is always a bath before bedtime and soap before meals.

Play with children... this is always more important that getting any housework done as kids grow up...and the housework will still need doing long after I'm dead and buried.

Enjoy a childhood... it's hard work at times... but fun.

I had a cleaner just because I prefer to play than dust.

Know what you are happy to do, capable of doing and just do the best you can within that remit.

Easy.

Nowadays, in this politically correct world we were supposed to say yes to everyone. This meant even if you did not feel competent to deal with some of the issues that may arise.

"...her foster carer has to go into hospital with another child she is looking after..."

Sarah had started to speak again. I wasn't really listening to what she said.

"...it's only going to be a six week placement. Just respite..."

I'd already spoken with Howard about this baby and we'd both agreed that it wasn't what we wanted to do.

Mia was just too damaged and had too many problems for me to cope with comfortably on a day to day basis.

I knew I couldn't look after her properly. What if I did something wrong and she died?

"...so you see Lorraine, there really is no-one other than you and Howard that I want to care for her."

I laughed and said I was used to social workers trying to get their placements in here and we happily obliged whenever we could; but this is just too much for us to cope with at the moment.

We were very lucky to have such a good reputation, though this often meant that a social worker would phone knowing we were full, but asking when one of our children or group of children would be moving out.

Or if we could just squeeze one more little head in.

This also meant we could, to an extent be choosey. If I knew a placement was coming to an end, I also phoned social workers that I liked working with (though there weren't that many of them) to let them know because, as far as I was concerned, if a foster carer and social worker got on, the placement would run smoothly, though not without the problems that the children and their birth family invariably bought with them.

Rarely did we have any time with just our 'home grown' children, though they never complained as they seemed to like having lots of children to play with as they grew up.

But this...this would be different.

This would be too different, too difficult and too much responsibility. We already had two children under the age of three years to care for and were working towards adoption for both of them. We had to consider the implications on them and their daily routines.

This was just not going to happen.

"Please Lorraine; it's only for six weeks. I'm her social worker so you know you can trust me. I'll be there anytime you need me and there is a huge support network already set up with the hospital and outside agencies."

"Besides" she said, "I know you. I trust you to do whatever it takes to help this baby and know you will manage."

Bugger it.

The trouble was Sarah was one of the few social workers I had worked with that I truly liked and trusted to work in a child's best interest.

She always listened to whatever information I had to give and, even if she didn't agree with my viewpoint, she considered it and, if warranted, would change her stance.

And, unfortunately; Sarah did know me...

"Aawww...Sarah!"

Sod it...I said the one word...just one word that I hadn't intended to...

"Okay"

And the rest is history...

"...so long as it's just six weeks. So long as I can phone you when you are at work and I need to know everything is okay. I don't want any bullshit about how good we are; I just want one hundred percent support from you."

I could almost see the smile swimming down the phone line.

Sarah sighed, "Thank you Lorraine. I'm on the other end of the phone and will call in as often as you want."

With that Sarah ended the phone call as she had to get the arrangements moving along.

Even as Sarah ended the call I knew; really knew, that with the best will in the world...she wouldn't always be at the end of the phone.

I knew she would and did have other caseloads that were equally as important as Mia...just not to me and my family.

Still, it was only for six weeks...

Chapter 2

Time was of the essence as the foster carer who was presently looking after Mia, was needed to go into hospital with another child she was caring for.

As I knew this carer I knew she would be rushed off her feet giving reassurance to the children she cared for about them going for a little holiday with nice people. Sharon only worked for the disability team so was very well placed to care for Mia.

Oh my God. What had I done?

Still, at the end of the day, six weeks is nothing, it's a walk in the park.

I should have thought though of all the other 'short' placements we'd had that had stretched out to months and even years, but I was now too busy with my own thoughts.

I had to let Howard know, so phoned him at work.

He was cool. Howard is always cool and accepts my fallibilities.

At that time I had no idea that by the end of this placement, more than any other child before or since, I would emerge such a different person...I would learn patience beyond anything I had ever known before and what true compassion was all about.

I would no longer fear disability or caring for a person with a disability.

But the biggest lesson I would learn is how one baby, one tiny scrawny little bag of bones, could move me to love her as though I had given birth to her myself.

How this scrawny little lady could move a community to offer support, even if only in a friendly greeting as we walked through the village.

How Mia, our beautiful Mia, could make my whole family go gooey eyed over the tiniest little thing she managed to do.

And sadly, I would learn what true hatred is all about...oh how I learned to hate this beautiful baby's mother...

Chapter 3

So here we are.

It's a beautiful sunny day early in August.

Fortunately our children are growing up and, with one living abroad; one married with children; one at university and the youngest getting ready to go later this year, our lives are quite nice and orderly.

We normally have between one and five children sharing our home as, some social workers consider three children to be just one count if they are a sibling group...so with five children taking up five beds...they can sometimes equate to just two placements.

It's kind of...the way social workers do their sums.

Anyway, back to where I was.

It's a lovely August day.

Mia is due at any time.

Mia is nasal tube fed; she is epileptic; she is on huge doses of medication and I believe she is possibly blind and there are definite signs of brain damage, caused by the savage shaking she received from one of her parents.

I'm me.

No-one special.

Certainly no-one that has had any training in this field, and I'm going to be her main carer.

Mia arrives just after lunchtime with Sharon and we sit and have a cup of tea while Sharon gives me some important information and gives Mia a feed.

I watched.

Shit...this is not what I signed up for.

Her next feed isn't due until about 1800.

Once Sharon has fed Mia it is time to bring all the things into our home that we will need to care for her.

As this is a respite placement we don't need to have everything she owns; but what we do get is amazing...

Boxes of feed; box after box of syringes, small syringes of varying sizes for her medication...larger ones for her feeds.

I don't need Mia's pram; cot or any bedding as I have them already.

The house is gradually being taken over with boxes and a case of Mia's clothes.

I am also given Mia's medication and the book that I need to log everything that Mia has and when she has it. Vitally important as we need to accurately record each dose of medicine, when she had it and how she was afterwards as well as what her feeds were and if it was a nasal or bottle feed...and of course, how she was after each feed.

Then Sharon leaves as she has to finalise details for her impending stay in hospital with her foster child.

I looked at Mia. She was so tiny. Not just tiny in length because she was a baby, but tiny around.

Mia was a truly scrawny little lady, with one end of a tube going up her nose and down her throat, the other end dangling down with an attachment for a syringe on the end so I could feed her. This tube was stuck to her face with micro pore tape.

Mia had short thick hair, too much for her tiny face, and eyes that moved all over the place without seeming to see anything. She made funny little mewing sounds most of the time and, when having an epileptic fit one or both of her arms would rise above her head and her eyes rolled. Sometimes I would learn, her little back would also arch, depending on the severity of the seizure she was going through.

And Mia could scream.

This is great, as first off, because I have no training in nasal gastro feeding it is too dangerous for me to feed her as I may inadvertently syringe the feed into her lungs. This could easily happen because, though the tube is inserted into her tummy, with a little cough it could move out of the tummy and slot into the lungs.

This means I have to go to the hospital to get training before her next feed.

Don't you just love the planning that goes into some jobs? The ideal situation would have been for me to spend some time prior to the start of the placement getting to know Mia, but I suppose there may have been a concern that I'd be scared off and turn this placement down and also, the time limit from deciding to run with this placement to it actually commencing just didn't allow for introductory visits from either me to Sharon or her to me.

Also...my God! The medicines this baby comes with means I have to beg my parent's spare lockable medicine cabinet as I can't find one large enough in the shops and there is quite a potent mixture of medication as well.

Our other two 'borrowed' children came in to see this noisy little newcomer, but she didn't hold their interest for long, such is the concentration of the under three's, so they crawled and waddled back out to play.

Jonathan was just eighteen months and soon to be placed with his adoptive family so we were going through the process of introductions at the moment.

Michael, aged two and such an adorable little man had been with us for a year. His mother tried very hard to care properly for him but, in all honesty, though I liked her a lot, I wouldn't leave a dead dog in her care. I would have liked to have had her as a placement when she was a little girl though, so she could have enjoyed the feeling of being parented appropriately instead of living through the sad childhood that she had. Maybe if someone had intervened early enough in her life things would now be different and she would now, as a young adult, have been able to make better life choices.

We were working towards adoption for Michael as well, though this would be some time the following year, or later.

Chapter 4

I went to the hospital that evening with Mia to learn how to do this nasal tube feeding.

No problem naively I think.

Pop in; let the nurses show me how it's done and leave...not.

First, I entered paediatric triage.

The nurses recognised Mia as they had spent so much time with her when she was first injured.

I explained who I was and that I had come to be shown how to tube feed and that she was due a feed now.

I also told them that I had seen Sharon feed her and noted that I had to expirate her before giving her anything. The expiratory procedure is where some fluid is drawn from the feeding tube and tested on a piece of litmus paper...providing it turns the right colour it is still in the tummy and okay to proceed with feeding...if it turns the wrong colour it means the tube has moved and will need to be put back in place at the hospital. This would happen many times over the coming months unfortunately.

So...the nurse carried out the expiratory procedure on Mia, and then started to feed her. Then I was left to give Mia the remainder of her feed under the watchful eyes of the nurses on duty.

All done, nappy changed, Mia is comfortable so I was off home.

But it doesn't happen like that.

I then had to stay at the hospital until her next feed at 1130 and do the whole thing myself so the nurses could see that I was competent.

Poor Howard had to cope with the whole evening routine at home on his own after a day in the office. I was and am so very lucky to have this wonderful and such caring man in my life.

I trundled home just after midnight so was in no happy wakey frame of mind the next morning.

Howard bought me a cup of coffee and let me know that all three children wanted attention and he was having to get ready for work so I had to get up and shower while he amused the boys and settled Mia as best he could.

This was going to be such a fun day.

First I had to return to the hospital for more feeding training then go to social services to meet Mia's mother and maternal grandmother and work out a care package that may result in this little lady returning to the nasty piece of work that may well have stolen her future from her.

I have to say that at this point I didn't know too much about what had happened to Mia except that she had been shaken by one of her parents. Which one of them had done this I didn't know.

All I did know was that I wouldn't want her returning to anyone who could do such a thing to such a tiny innocent child, or stand by while someone else did and do nothing to stop it.

There would never be a first day at play school making new friends; no first day at infant school where she could run happily into a new class; no brownies; no guides; no boyfriends with the tears and laughter that goes with all of that; no engagement, marriage and children of her own...no magical future for her.

Just an existence where she would always need someone to do the most basic things we all take for granted. Having said that I am an optimist so held on the thought that maybe, just maybe she would improve with time.

The hospital visit was fine. The nurses, though different from last night all knew Mia and what had happened to her, so made a huge fuss and let me head home after a few hours.

Before going to the meeting I popped home to see the children who had been happily oblivious to my absence thanks to my dear friend and co foster carer Elizabeth and her fostered children.

Like us, Elizabeth had been fostering for fourteen years and her children had now grown up, though not quite flown the nest like ours had. She was a dab hand at looking after any number of children and we often shared the childcare between us when either of us had to attend meetings, so all my children, home grown or not, knew her and her family well.

Once I'd had some lunch and fed Mia I was ready to shoot off to meet the mother and grandmother. Not something I was looking forward to as, from what I'd heard, this little lady's injuries could be down to me as this mother could certainly re-write history.

I reassured Elizabeth that I would be home before Mia needed another feed and set off.

Neither of us knew at that point, that soon Elizabeth and her family would be going through the same process as we were, as they had a baby boy placed with them some weeks later who had gone through similar torment as Mia.

Chapter 5

I walked into the office with Sarah, chatting about how things had gone since Mia arrived. She took me to one side and explained that the mother and grandmother were in a side office waiting to 'interview' me to ascertain if I was a good enough foster carer to look after a baby with such special needs.

Oh this just sounds great.

On entering the room I saw a rather mousy looking woman sitting next to who was quite obviously the grandmother.

Both of them looked at me.

And then the interview began...what was my experience with looking after children; had I ever looked after a child with special needs (don't all children have them?); had I ever tube fed before; was Mia settled; do I have my own family; do I drive; what sort of car do I have and does it have 'air-con'...Air-con, what the hell was that? The mother explained...air conditioning. Ah, yes it does. I made a mental note to try to find out as many abbreviations as possible for future conversations, and of course, to remember that one. The mother was still talking; will

I work towards getting her back to her mother's home...on and on they asked questions and watched...

I also watched.

The mother's eyes were so hard and spiteful. She appeared to be quite an emotionless woman, much the same as the grandmother who seemed quite 'hard' and angry with the world in general. I had gone into the meeting with an open mind but was starting to form opinions already. When the mother didn't think anyone was watching, her mask dropped, and the evil just slipped right back where it belonged; deep in her soul with just a glint from her eyes.

Oh dear...I'm judging and don't even know these people yet. But I do know what I've been told by various people that have been involved with this family from the start so my judgement is based on solid ground.

The mother's voice was emotionless as well...just flat.

The grandmother also appeared to be quite emotionless and exonerated the mother of any wrongdoing.

Oh yes, they both made it clear that the mother had done nothing wrong and should have Mia home as soon as possible.

I know we are not supposed to make judgements on people but, these two were not the usual sort of people I came into contact with via the office as clients.

These were educated people. People that had been given a chance in life...not from some sink estate where there is little escape from the depravation all around them.

They should have known better.

I also knew better, so made a conscious decision that I would get on with the mother as she may actually be the innocent one in this sorry mess and just because someone looks angry, hard and emotionless doesn't mean they are.

Once my interview was over we got on to discussing the plan of action regarding Mia.

At the end of the meeting I was given a copy of the placement request form. This clearly stated that Mia had received brain damage due to a none accidental head injury and that her father had been charged with causing this injury...it also had written clearly under the heading of Duration of Placement...not yet known...until first review.

We had no dates planned yet for when that review would be. I should have queried this but said nothing.

Chapter 6

Mia was to have supervised contact with the mother three times a week, starting the day after I had met the mother and grandmother. These were, where possible to be at times when she wouldn't need a feed though, as the mother had not received any training in giving nasogastric feeds.

We were also asked at this time, as well as tube feeding; to try to get Mia on to bottle feeds...

We were to try giving a little normality to an extraordinary baby.

Now, bottle feeding Mia proved to be quite a challenge.

First, she had the tube to contend with down her throat. This alone must have made taking anything orally feel odd. Also, there was always the possibility that the feeds would go down the wrong way and end up in her lungs.

But...

I'd been told to try to feed her whenever possible so I did...

And she was sick.

Mia would sometimes take a feed and down it went and stayed down. Other times, in fact most times, it came back up with such a vengeance that whenever I was feeding her we had to take the other children from the room, spread towels all over the floor and hope for the best. The best sometimes being that she only threw back a little milk...the worse was when she threw back everything, projectile vomiting over a three metre area!

And then of course there were the times when she would be so violently sick that the tube would be sent flying out of her mouth and we would have to gently ease it out from her nose and return to the hospital so it could be put back again. Not something I was qualified to do as it could easily be inserted into her lungs instead of her tummy.

But we persevered for weeks, if a feed was thrown back, I then had to tube her to make sure she was not going to waste away, and, to be honest, she couldn't afford to lose any weight at that time.

Also, most concerning was the thought that every time a feed was vomited back, she was also possibly losing some of the various medicines that had been administered...something she could ill afford to do.

I was now trying to look after two lively little boys and keep on top of an ever growing mountain of towels that needed laundering!

Due to the amount Mia could throw back following a feed I was also having to wash down walls and doors as well as furniture...in fact; everything that was in the room came in for scrupulous scrubbing on a daily basis (including me).

Chapter 7

Mia had been with us for three days when I first ventured out on my own with her.

Howard was home for the weekend and offered to look after Jonathon and Michael on the Saturday morning so I could take Mia to visit my parents.

My parents live at the other end of our village so I had a nice leisurely stroll to their home with Mia sleeping peacefully in the pram. Both of my parents made such a fuss over her when she woke, giving her cuddles and cooing at her.

This was lovely because when we had first discussed fostering children my parents, and my mother in particular, had been unhappy with our decision, feeling that our children would miss out on a 'normal' childhood. They had nonetheless been excellent grandparents to all the children that had joined our family for varying lengths of time.

Both Howard and I had been so happy when both our parents, regardless of their initial concerns, had treated all our borrowed children as though we had given birth to them ourselves; Christmas, Easter and birthdays had, over the years proved quite an expensive time for them as no child was ever forgotten or bought an inferior present to those purchased for their birth grandchildren.

I wished Howards parents were still here as I knew they would also make a big fuss of this little lady, as they had all of our borrowed children, but they had both died a couple of years ago and were so sadly missed.

Once I had spent about an hour and a half with my parents I set off for home as Mia would be needing her next feed.

Mia was settled and asleep in the pram as I slowly enjoyed the walk home. Quite a few people who knew me stopped me to admire Mia as I walked along, commenting that it must be nice to have a tiny baby join our family again.

No-one failed to notice the tube going up Mia's nose and I explained to those that asked that Mia needed tube feeding at the moment due to illness.

As luck would have it I was walking past the one shop that sold baby bedding when Mia woke.

Mia didn't only wake though. Mia's eyes opened at the same time as her mouth and she was sick.

Mia was so sick she covered the inside of the pram. She was lying in a huge puddle of warm sticky creamy coloured liquid. Her hair and face were a mass of goo...her clothes kind of stuck to her little body...arms; legs; feet...what a mess!

There was nothing in the pram that wasn't soaking wet and smelling of...well, of baby puke that wasn't quite baby puke.

And then Mia started to scream.

I went into the shop and had to buy new sheets for the pram and the staff helped me as I stripped Mia out of her clothes by cleaning the pram for me, putting the soiled bedding in the bag and mopping the mattress and sides of the pram before putting the clean sheets in place.

Half an hour later and I was home with Mia naked apart from her nappy, asleep in a clean pram.

Luckily it was a lovely hot day and the need for Mia to be dressed beautifully was mine alone.

Chapter 8

As a family, we would have to get used to the amount of hospital appointments Mia had, sorting out child care for the boys and juggling meetings to fit everything in, for though it was only to be a respite placements appointments still needed to be kept and made for the future.

Mia needed to see the dietician to get her tube feeds as these were specialised formula with extra nutritional values; she had to see her paediatrician to ensure the medicinal regime she was on was still working for her...her fits changed so her medication would be changed; something added and something taken away.

She also had to see the occupational therapy team; someone from education; our regular doctor; the district nurse when call out necessitated; paediatric outpatients; Doctor Frankie; the ophthalmologist; our family doctor and the health visitor as well as seeing the team that supported her from Great Ormond Street hospital.

It was early days for her because, though she had been born beautiful and healthy, at four weeks old she had apparently been so badly shaken that her injuries were considered to be consistent with being in a high speed car crash without wearing any restraint.

She was now six months old and, though still beautiful, she was no longer healthy and all we could do was hope that a miracle would happen and she would finally become the child she was born to be.

It took me many months before I accepted she was epileptic.

Sure she had fits, but that didn't mean she had to have a label.

Even I had to concede that it was a label she would need, if only to ensure she got the right support.

Chapter 9

Seven months before Mia came to share our home Howard and I had become proud grandparents for the second time, thanks to our son Edward and his wife Louise.

We now had two granddaughters; Jade and Mia.

Mia was a month older than our new addition so we had Mia and Mia in our home quite often.

We tried Mia one and Mia two.

That didn't work.

Jade, who was just two but quite vocal, found it easier to say "grannies Mia" when referring to our new arrival, so we stuck with that.

It was only going to be for six weeks after all.

When Louise came to greet our new little lady we placed both babies on the floor next to each other.

They were both about the same size and the same build.

Six and seven months old respectively they were both doing the same thing.

Just lying there.

Then my granddaughter smiled and reached up towards her mother's face.

Mia just lay there; mostly unresponsive, though turned her head toward noise while her eyes darted all over the place.

I figured we could assess some of Mia's progress by whatever our granddaughter was doing as they were so close in age.

This was in many ways to prove a heart breaking exercise.

We were to find in the weeks and then months that followed, as our granddaughter started to roll over and reach for toys, Mia still just lay on the floor not reaching for anything, just turning her head towards sounds around her.

If our granddaughter was in her bouncy chair reaching for toys, Mia would be in hers, not knowing the toys were dangling in front of her unless we put her hand on them...then she would let go as soon as you removed your hand.

When our granddaughter started to sit; then walk and run, we had to concede that Mia really was in a very bad way.

Finally we had to acknowledge what we all knew to be true. What we had known really since she had arrived in our home, occupying a small cot and claiming a big part of our hearts.

Mia did not have the future that our granddaughter and countless other children her age; older and younger had.

Edward, Louise, Jade and Mia were frequent visitors to our home, living only a few streets away and fortunately we are a close family and all get on well together.

Louise gradually became my main support worker by doing most of the childcare I needed when Mia had to go to hospital which was quite often and mostly unplanned.

Louise, being the wonderful and capable young woman that she is also took time to learn as much as possible about our Mia and her routine. Louise is very much like me in that she doesn't panic easily and has a fairly laid back approach to life. Because of the commitment Louise had always shown to our 'borrowed' children I had no concerns when she looked after Mia if I had meeting to attend that I couldn't take her to.

Caring for Mia was something the whole family became involved in, even my parents spent more time helping out than ever before, and they had always been 'on tap' so to speak.

The only parts of caring for Mia that was exclusively mine was giving her the huge amounts of medication that she needed three times a day and giving feeds when she was nasal tube fed, so whatever I was doing had to be arranged around that.

Chapter 10

I very quickly found that when we went out and about in our village that Mia was quite well known. This was in part because we were regular church goers and, on the first Sunday Mia had attended with us our minister, such a lovely kind lady, had come to see who had joined our family.

She was clearly upset when she saw Mia and though bound by the constraints of confidentiality, I told her that Mia had been the victim of a none accidental head injury. At the end of the service, when all the children returned from their various Sunday school activities and the youngest came in from the crèche, Mia was taken in the ministers arms and introduced to the congregation.

Everyone welcomed her as she was taken around the church, so I suppose members of our congregation had spoken of her to their friends and, though they didn't know the details of what had happened to her, they knew she was one poorly little lady.

People would come up to say hello to her whenever we were out and gently stroke her face, something she reacted to in a positive way, which was nice.

Also, Howard and I are well known as we'd fostered for such a long time and had such an assortment of children join and leave our family, people just came over to see who had now come to share our home life.

I didn't get any pitying looks because of Mia's disabilities; just gentle hands stroking Mia on her face or arm, sometimes a gentle hand would hold hers with gentle cooing sounds aimed towards her.

Much later, when Mia had been with us for almost two years, my sister would take her for a walk to the shops and, in every shop she went into she was stopped by a member of staff and questioned as to what her relationship was with Mia...everyone looked out for her and wanted to know she was safe.

My sister even had a member of the public approach her and ask what she was doing with Mia...it was the only time she ever asked to take her out on her own as it took too long to get around and do her twenty minute shop.

I never did a twenty minute shop.

I always met too many people to talk to.

Chapter 11

As a fostering family we had been quite lucky in many ways that our home address had been kept private from most of the families whose children we looked after.

Sure, we had home contact with some of them but, those the department considered too threatening to us or any member of our family had not been given our address and had contact in the family suite run by social services.

This was one of the families that would not be getting it. The reason wasn't because anyone in my family would be at risk of physical violence, but over concerns that the mother may make up malicious stories about me and how I was caring for Mia if there wasn't a social worker overseeing the contact sessions. Every malicious story takes up valuable social worker and foster carer time being investigated so it was a wise choice for the department to make.

But, the department isn't infallible and due to a little oversight unintentionally, only a few weeks into this placement, gave paperwork to the family that contained details of where we lived.

The department paid out for high fencing to be put around our garden...we already had panic buttons on the front and back doors and CCTV as a deterrent very visible out the front.

These precautions unfortunately didn't stop us getting a bullet hole in the glass of our door while we had been looking after another little family though...But that is another story...

We didn't think that Mia's family would cause a problem by having this information, but we wanted to be able to relax in our garden without the chance of them turning up and trying to look in or follow us if we walked to the shops or parks.

Even with all the precautions we had in place to ensure every child that shared our home would be safe living with us, I wasn't happy with the department for letting our address be known to the birth family. If foster carers do something wrong, irrespective of it being 'accidental', they know about it and can face disciplinary action and be sacked. This was a serious breach of protocol, an action that could have placed a child in danger and mean the child has to have a change of placement in order to keep them safe. I only had to hope that the financial outlay by the department meant they would be more careful with future placements they made when an address had to be withheld from the birth family, but was too grateful for them for not moving Mia to do more about it.

Contact was happening three times a week which Mia's mother and sometimes the grandmother attended. This usually resulted in some complaint or other; Mia had a dirty nappy when she arrived for contact (like I could stop her soiling en-route); she was sick over the mother (that I loved); she slept; she cried; she had a fit; she was too hot; she was too cold; mother didn't like the colour clothes or the style clothes Mia was wearing. The list was endless.

Sometimes the mother complained I packed too much; most times she complained I packed too little and the complaint would be that the mother had run out of baby wipes.

Mia usually had at least thirty wipes in her contact bag and a dozen nappies and nappy sacks. But experience had taught me that parents often have scant regard for items sent with their children to contact and quite often the wipes would be used to mop up any spills even if they are not caused by their child...just so the wipes are used, or of course, sometimes they just took the items home with them so the contact bag came back empty and I had to do a total restock for the next contact session.

All these complaints were quite pathetic but all needed to be acknowledged none the less.

The mother also complained if Mia had to be admitted to hospital, which though infrequent at this time, did happen on a number of occasions if her epilepsy became unstable and her medication had to be monitored closely when being changed.

These times were also frustrating for our family as I couldn't spend all day with her, partly due to looking after the other children we cared for and partly due to the mother having contact. I had as little contact with the mother as possible because relations had very quickly gone downhill in that quarter, following a telephone conversation I'd had with her one evening.

Howard and I had been relaxing after the children had all gone to bed when the mother phoned. During the conversation I'd told her that Mia didn't appear to enjoy a particular toy…the mother then told me it could be because Mia had some memory of what had happened to her. I told her that I didn't know what had happened and she said quite flippantly "Oh…she was strangled; suffocated and shaken then received about five or six blows to the head". The mother went on to say she knew because Mia's father had told her what he had done and that the police knew she hadn't done anything but social services were 'doing' her for neglect. She also asked me why I was always nice to her. I let her know it was my job to be nice to people and that it was not my job to judge her, but to care for Mia and make sure she was safe.

I didn't lie when I said that it wasn't my job to judge her because that part was true…I just didn't tell her that unfortunately I had no choice but to evaluate her not only by her actions but also by Mia's reactions towards her.

I had my opinions regarding her and her actions and though I didn't voice them to many people involved in the case I claimed them as my own, as I do to date, though what other people thought and think is down to them.

Chapter 12

Mia had been with us for three weeks when I had the first of many appointments with Doctor Frankie.

I had known Doctor Frankie for many years as she was the paediatric doctor favoured by social services, and was very much a hands-on doctor who I had enjoyed a positive relationship with for most of my fostering career. It's always better if you are able to relax and share information relevant to a case with someone you respect a great deal and knowing that respect is reciprocated.

Mia was checked over by Doctor Frankie and her medication slightly changed...one of many changes that would happen over the course of time.

I was also advised at this time that it was probably best to stick with tube feeding until she could be assessed at Great Ormond Street regarding where her feeds go when using the bottle. Perhaps she was being sick because it was going straight into her lungs.

With reluctance I stopped bottle feeds straight away.

Mia had lost the joy of seeing everyday things; the sky; the grass; the faces and smiles of those that had already grown to love her.

Now, Mia had once again lost the joy of taste.

To make sure Mia always knew it was me when I approached her I made sure to only wear one perfume...Channel No 5. No-one else I mixed with used this so it was a good one to go with and it was nice to see at least one small reaction and a calming come over her whenever I was near if I wasn't talking to her. I tried always to talk when I was around Mia. If she was sleeping I would just speak quietly, saying what I was doing, or I would sing (no, I'm not that good but Mia and the boys didn't seem to mind).

I also spoke every time I entered a room she was in, even if I'd only popped out for a moment, so she knew it was me, and if Mia was having a fit I would gently stroke her face or arm and whisper quietly to her so she knew she was not alone in that dark space she went to, that I didn't even know if I could reach.

Dear God...I was starting to have such strong feeling for Mia.

This can't be happening...she's only been with us a few weeks.

I pushed them back...tried to shut them off because she was only going to be here for a few more weeks and then my life would return to normal.

All our lives would return to normal.

I wasn't aware then that our son James had already spoken about Mia to his siblings.

It would be many, many months before they told me that he had said Mia would never leave our family because we all loved her too much and, "mum will never be able to let her go."

Chapter 13

At the end of September, after Mia had been with us for just five weeks I attended an appointment with the physiotherapy team.

I had arrived at the hospital and was asked to wait in one of the rooms used by the team. There were quite a few seats in the room, set out in a circle.

This was to be a professionals meeting to decide which direction we would be going with Mia regarding her exercise regime. Her birth family were not included in this meeting but would be given copies of any routine Mia was going to be following so they could also be involved during their contact sessions.

Anyway, there I was, sitting on a chair with Mia on my lap. I had found that if I sat with Mia's back against my body and supported her with one arm around her front, leaving one had free to caress her arms, legs, face and hands, she relaxed.

So that's how we were sitting when the physiotherapist walked into the room.

She stopped in the doorway and just starred.

I knew the right way normally to hold a baby was cradled in my arms or with her head on my shoulder and supporting her back with one arm whilst the other secured her below her bottom, so immediately felt like I had done something wrong from the look on her face.

Her eyes seemed to widen and her mouth opened. Then she just told me not to move...stay exactly like I was...she had to go get the rest of the team right away.

Shit...nothing to do but sit still and wait.

Well, the team came in and suddenly the room was filled with smiling faces.

The team were all talking as they walked across the room and a few knelt down in front of me and I swear there were a few damp eyes in that room.

Then Mary, the head physiotherapist said "I've known Mia since this happened and I've never seen her with her hands opened. She just looks so relaxed. And she's gained weight."

Wow. My eyes misted up. Things were going well for Mia.

I wanted to cry tears of joy, but swallowed back...must stay professional...Mia is not my baby, she is someone else's.

One day soon she would be someone else's 'problem'.

Even as I thought these awful thoughts, I knew I didn't believe them.

How could I?

I loved this child.

No you don't...you just think you do.

You just pity her.

You pity her...but you don't want other people to pity her...to pity you...

Sod it.

Concentrate woman.

You will never let this baby go.

Mmm...Oh yes I will...

My heart already knew what my head refused to acknowledge yet.

We had made a positive difference to Mia. She was content. She showed her contentment and I'd never noticed this tiny miracle happen in the 'normality' of our chaotic everyday family life.

I hadn't realised the significance of that tiny movement.

I couldn't even remember when she had opened her little fist the first time; though I could remember that her hands used to be sweaty and moist when she first arrived. How I'd had to massage her tiny hands to get them to open just the tiniest little bit so I could wash them. How they used to have the smell of sweat in them...it seemed so long ago. Other events had made me forget these small jobs that I'd had to do. I wondered if I had let other memories slip away as Mia had settled into our family.

As Mia had become one of our family.

I think that was possibly when the decision to leave Mia with us was first considered...the physiotherapist must have spoken to the social worker about how relaxed and settled Mia was and a seed was sown...

We just weren't aware of it.

I thank God, even now, for helping Mia to let everyone know she was happy and settled since coming to live with our family.

Following the meeting I was shown how to massage Mia's legs and how to give her back massages that would make her more comfortable.

Before each meal Mia needed to have a back massage that would loosen up any mucus and hopefully she would bring this up, enabling her then to keep her feed down. If possible it would be good to give her another back massage shortly after her feed, though allowing time for her to digest what she'd had first. We knew that to give a massage too soon after feeding and she would bring everything back up.

I was also shown how to pick Mia up; total body contact at all times. This meant that if Mia was lying down I was to gently lie across her as I scooped her up. This was to let her know that she was safe.

Only thing was, from day one I had treated Mia as a normal baby. To me, her disability was secondary to the child she was.

Mia was a baby with a disability; not a disabled baby.

I spoke to her whenever I was with her. I sang nursery rhymes to her and the boys all the time.

I told her everything I was doing as though she understood, which of course, she probably didn't. She was only seven months old after all. But this is what I had always done, even with our own children when they were babies.

She had shown she was contented, so to change how I treated her now would maybe cause distress so, though I listened, I knew I would continue as I had started. After all, I figured that if I were to do all that I was advised I'd end up with back and hip problems and how much use would I be then?

As we were nearing the end of the six week period I decided I would make as few calls as possible to social services regarding Mia, figuring that as I hadn't heard anything about Mia returning to Sharon in the near future and appointments having been made for various outside agencies to visit Mia at our home…perhaps she would be staying a little longer and I didn't want anyone remembering that this had started out as a short term respite placement.

I think the department were possibly thinking the same, as they had stopped calling me so often and were leaving me to get on with the day to day task of bringing up three pre-school children in the knowledge that I would call them if I needed to.

Chapter 14

Two weeks later I met her man from education.

Tom.

What on earth could an eight month old baby want with a man from education?

I was about to be educated, and what an eye opener it was.

Tom arrived on time. He was over six feet tall and dressed in a relaxed fashion.

Tom looked much like a university professor. He had on a tweedy jacket, casual trousers and loafers. Nothing like I'd expected him to look. Everything about Tom was relaxed and gentle and though I would, in the future sometimes get frustrated with the things he wanted us to do in encouraging Mia's progression, while he was here there was a calmness that was comforting.

He came in chatting to me and Mia, gently stroking her hand as he spoke.

Mia was soon nicely relaxed and so was I.

This bodes well I thought.

We would go on to have an excellent working relationship until Tom left to work at Great Ormond Street the following year.

Tom told me that Mia had been part of his caseload since she was four months old and went on to explain the importance of sensory input. He suggested raising her awareness of light by moving her towards and away from the window, putting artificial lights on and off while noting her responses and by shining a torch onto reflective surfaces. We were also to try developing her sense of anticipation by touch songs and games and to have different songs sung at different times of the day so she would associate them with what was happening next, such as meal times and bath or bed times.

He helped to design a sensory corner for Mia in the play room, where she would spend most of her time. But, it was to be moveable so we could have it in any room we were in; this also meant it could go in the garden or to friends' homes when we visited.

Tom explained that though it appeared like Mia was blind...she could probably still tell light from dark. We would get a light tube that changed colours...when we did it was five feet tall!

Tom also discussed the importance of textures...we would need soft; itchy; hard and crinkly materials.

Then there was the importance of sound...an Indian rain maker; rattles; soft music and bells.

Tom and I chatted about the size needed to make a sensory corner. It didn't need to be huge, just big enough for Mia to lie in with everything close enough for her to touch if she moved her arms...though the only times Mia appeared to move anything was when she had a fit as far as I could see. She had never reached for anything or actually held anything since she moved in unless it had been placed directly into her hand and then she tended to let go of it as soon as the supporting hand was moved away. Still, there was always tomorrow.

Tom came every couple of weeks over the coming months to see Mia and catch up with what was happening in her life. He bought a box with him on one of these visits for us to use as a sensory toy, the idea being that she is placed with it around her which would block out some external noise, but she didn't like that...I knew because she became distressed when it was used. I tried to imagine what it must be like...a dark world full of noise, and then that noise quietened. I think I would feel scared, familiarity, even if only sound, is comforting after all.

What we did next was purchase a large playpen. It had to be one with a gate as I couldn't take the chance of dropping Mia if I was trying to lower her into it nor of damaging my back as she got heavier. Also, as by now we knew she wasn't going to be living anywhere else but with our family for the foreseeable future, it had to be something easily adaptable for her as she grew so we got one that could even be used as a room divider which would give her more space in the future.

When this sensory corner was complete there were different textures for Mia to be laid on, noisy and brightly coloured toys hung above her and lay beside her. There was a reflective board attached to one side and a cover to go over the whole lot to make it dark for when we were doing her 'light and dark' exercises. The light tube, when we purchased it some months down the road, was the only item we couldn't take around where ever we went, and would be placed near her head so she would get any benefit from the different shades as they glided up and down and feel the soft vibration of the motor when it was on.

By now Mia was becoming more responsive and was vocalising. Mia had begun making cooing sounds when she woke to let us know her day had started and appeared to be responding to 'anticipation songs' such as round and round the garden. Repetition is a wonderful thing for learning and I was learning that this is even more important when the child you are teaching has such profound disabilities. We were also now trying to establish a routine of activities for Mia so she could have more relaxed time perhaps knowing what would be happening next. Her response to games like 'round and round the garden' and 'horsey horsey' was also good and, though Mia didn't laugh or smile, her reaction in remaining calm during the game and becoming slightly distressed when it ended was indication for everyone that she had been having fun.

Mia's first review meeting came and went and, with Mia responding to the targets that had been set by the physiotherapists and occupational therapist everyone apart from the mother and grandmother were happy with the care and support Mia was receiving. The mother was content however for Mia to remain with us rather than be placed with another fostering family or return to Sharon who, for some reason they had taken a disliking towards at this time.

Another benefit for Mia was that Jonathon had now moved to his adoptive family and we were moving forward with Michael's adoption as well.

Soon there would be just Mia, Howard and me at home.

Mia would have our undivided attention.

Life would get easier for everyone.

****

As a rule our doctors are very good...a couple of them are absolutely excellent and the same can be said for our receptionists, especially one who was going to prove a Godsend in helping to sort out prescriptions and appointments for Mia and all the children we had after her...so they are not all like the 'little Hilters' so many people complain about.

We were very fortunate also to have an excellent chemist very close to our home, though I only discovered this by chance one day because, following the meeting with Tom I had spotted a lovely play mat in the window on the way to the doctors and thought I'd buy it for Mia on the way home, instead of going to chemist in the High Street as was usual. I popped Mia's prescription over the counter and continued to browse around the shop while I waited. I didn't have to wait long before being called to the counter. As the young pharmacist handed me the medication and instructions on how to use it she saw

Mia in the pram, looking lovely as always. She noticed the tube and probably because of the medication I'd just been given mentioned how poorly Mia must be, she then pointed out some other items in their toy section that may be useful in stimulating Mia because they either, vibrated, made lovely sounds or were very brightly coloured. This was the start of a very good relationship with Carrie and from that day on I always popped prescriptions in for her to fill.

A couple of months passed and I was chatting to Carrie as I handed over another prescription...she looked at it and told me she couldn't fill this one for me as it was for a strength ten times too strong for Mia. I looked at her as she said if she gave me them just one dose would be enough to kill her. I went back to the surgery and waited while another prescription was made out then returned to get the medicines.

Carrie just laughed when I handed it over and asked me what doctor I had seen and wasn't amused when I told her we had seen a locum as our doctor was on holiday. This time the prescription was so weak that it wouldn't do anything and Mia would possibly have had major fits within a day or so.

Carrie phoned our surgery and luckily spoke to Jennifer who was quite appalled at the mistake and said she would get another prescription filled and sent to the chemist to save me having to walk the mile back there again, which she did...but it was yet another wrong dose so it took a few more phone calls between Carrie and Jennifer (and I think Jennifer then stood over the doctor while he wrote the prescription out properly) before we finally got home.

We were lucky this never happened again and I was pleased to have these two special ladies keeping an eye on Mia's prescriptions from then on.

Chapter 15

By the time Mia had shared our home and hearts for three months she was appearing much healthier than when she had first arrived and was clearly putting on weight. The decision to re-introduce bottle feeds had been made which meant she no longer required tube feeding. Having started with nasogastric feeding when Mia arrived we had managed to get her totally on to bottles; only for her to have a large epileptic fit and go back on tube feeds.

We had yo-yoed between bottle and tube feeds for a little while but Mia had now been tube fed for the past five weeks.

It was great to get rid of that damn tube. Without the tube it meant other people could feed Mia, making it easier for me to spend time playing with Michael, do household chores, cook and of course attend the many meetings I had to attend where I couldn't take her with me, without having to dash home in order to give her a meal, or arriving late as I'd been delayed due to needing to feed her.

It was also just so lovely to see Mia moving her lips in anticipation of a feed when her bottle was shook near her.

Proper feeds also (rather selfishly) meant I wouldn't be the one mopping everything up if I wasn't there... Fortunately our wonderful daughter-in-law Louise never seemed to mind if I dashed off after feeding Mia and having most of the feed thrown back all over the place...leaving her to clear up any gooey mess as well as look after all the children, but I felt guilty about it...if I wasn't there I wouldn't know if there was any mopping up to be done and my guilt would have no-where to reside. I felt blessed that our son had found such a loving, kind and capable young woman to spend his life with.

Of course, proper feeds would also mean that the mother could actively be involved with this part of Mia's routine and could start to possibly bond with her. I still didn't know if I would be happy at this change in activities but had to work to the care plan regardless of personal feelings.

I got the bottles and also following advice, started to give her solids.

This was progress. I can't think of many things I like more than the taste of delicious food and drinks. Now Mia was getting something else apart from touch and smell.

Now she really gained weight...Lots of weight.

This feeding regime had been interrupted briefly when Mia was admitted to hospital following an epileptic episode which was quite severe and she had refused all feeds by the nurses so they had no choice but to revert to tube feeding, but once settled back at home she was straight back on the bottle and solids.

Mia was also by now quite comfortable sitting up supported by me or another member of our family while we went through her daily routines. Sitting upright had been the recommended position to use when encouraging exploration with her hands and was also more effective for sound location.

Mia had also turned herself over a couple of times, though this distressed her it was a huge step forward as it showed she had the capability to move, which was exciting for everyone to know.

When Mia was gently touched she would respond positively and she appeared to recognise voices, turning towards people as they spoke to each other, but tended to keep her head facing those voices she knew if we had friends visiting.

During one of our visits from Tom he suggested that as part of Mia's meal time routine I should rattle the spoon against the bowl to encourage her to explore her food, even putting her hands into the food so she could check out the textures...unfortunately that was one suggestion I couldn't take on board...Tom clearly didn't have to clear up after mucky children's meals!

By the time Mia had lived with us for four months her weight had increased from below 0.4th to 9th centile. Her length was now on the second centile but sadly her head was just below the 0.4th centile. Her eye contact was still poor as they tended to dart all over the place but she was now responding more to vocal stimulation so it was thought that at least her hearing was working satisfactory.

Mia had also stopped drooling (another thing that had happened without me noticing) and she had started to baby babble, especially when she woke in the morning…it was just as though she wanted us to know she was ready for the day ahead.

Mia still made no attempt to reach for any toys which were within her reach so we didn't know if she could play with any of her toys that had visual stimulus like the coloured lights or bright and flashing lights, though if she knocked one by accident she would then knock it again several times, she just couldn't pick it up, though would now hold onto small items for short periods of time if they were placed in her hands. One toy that Mia did appear to enjoy was her piano…we had given it to her for Christmas. This piano could be either tied to the side of a cot or placed under the baby's feet. We placed it under Mia's feet and she would quite deliberately kick away, often aiming for the same key over and over again.

The only negative apart from the epilepsy was Mia's head control which was still poor, meaning she needed to have head support when she was sitting unlike other babies of her age.

It was also unfortunate for Mia, as with many other children and adults who have a neurological status of not moving very much, that she suffered badly with constipation which caused her a lot of distress at times, so needed daily medicinal support to enable her to open her bowels and keep her stools soft.

Mia was also still suffering from reflux and would start to cough when she was moved, something else that was distressing not only for her, but for everyone involved in her care. This was at least made easier with medication and at last her epileptic episodes were starting to be greatly reduced which was a huge relief and a bonus for everyone.

All these issues were quite normal for Mia so, apart from concerns regarding her liver function for which she had to have regular blood tests in order to have that monitored...things were finally starting to look up. Mia was responding to all the input from the support team that surrounded her.

After living with us for almost six months Mia was checked over by her paediatrician who reported that her weight had moved from the 9th centile to the 50th centile in just six weeks! It was just a shame her poor head was still on the 0.4th centile and didn't appear to be growing very much at all...so now we were heading towards Christmas and the New Year with a lot of positives behind us and only a few negatives.

Chapter 16

Life rarely happens the way we pen it out to.

Seven months had passed now. Our first Christmas with Mia had come and gone with everyone helping her to open presents and feel her new toys and clothes, and she'd celebrated her first birthday as part of our family which had been lovely, again everyone had given her brightly coloured and noisy toys that were the right size for us to place in her hands. Spring was peeping around the corner and Michael was now settling in with his lovely forever family.

All was peaceful at home.

Mia continued to thrive though she still had lots of appointments to attend at our local hospital; Great Ormond Street Hospital; the clinic and of course as an outpatient of her wonderful paediatrician, Doctor Frankie.

Contact continued with Mia's mother. Her mother was having two hours of contact three times a week and she now had supervised contact with her dad happening once a week. What was commented on by everyone who witnessed the contact between Mia and her dad was how, every time she was with her mother she would either sleep or become fretful, yet when with her dad she would settle and, even if awake, stay calm.

Personally, I think she shouted out to the world where she felt safest. But this is of course only my opinion.

So, with life nice and peaceful I had lots of time to give to Mia and trying to get her into a good routine of feeds and exercise.

Then I got a phone call.

Chapter 17

Could we please look after two children? They were boys…and oh how I loved having little boys around the house. Boys always seemed more relaxed and spontaneous in almost everything they did… especially in sharing their cuddles.

The answer was yes before I could say no. We were so used to a busy home with lots of noise and movement and cooking for more than just two people. Now with Michael, like Jonathon, settling in with his lovely new family our home was quiet. Our home was just too quiet.

Part of me wanted a child that would distract me from the enormity that was Mia. For love her as I did, the responsibility was sometimes just too big to comprehend…and the fears for her future, just too terrible.

Of course the social worker then went on to give me all the relevant information I needed to make sure everyone and everything was prepared for the children's arrival.

One sentence was uttered.

"The baby has been in hospital. He has been shaken by one of his parents but we don't know which one".

Didn't this social worker know we had Mia?

Oh yes, she knew. She also knew how Mia had thrived since being with us and hoped little Peter would do so as well.

Another little sentence was uttered.

"We think Carl is on the autistic spectrum".

Bloody hell!

Anything else while I'm sitting here or can I pick myself up from the floor now?

But I had already said yes to this placement and knew we would remain committed to looking after these little boys for as long as we were needed to.

We were also so very lucky that they had the most amazing grandparents, who offered untold support to us by remaining committed to the children and having them to stay for weekends as well as longer holidays whenever they were asked…though they rarely had to be asked as the offer to have the boys stay was usually being made by them.

Peter and Carl arrived the following day so we had the evening to get everything ready; bed made; cot made; cuddly toy left on each; tooth brushes brought and a change of night and day clothes as even though they were coming from another emergency carer, past placements had taught us they would need something new.

Carl, aged just over two and a half, gave me a total baptism of fire when he arrived...he was dragged in kicking and screaming...he did not like change or the 'stranger' in front of him!

He spat at me...he spat at everything and I learnt from him that if you cry and scream while you have your fingers up your nose...you produce copious amounts of phlegmy liquids and can produce an effect over everything like something out of 'Ghost Busters.' Carl also kicked; punched; pinched and, if you were that close he would bite as hard as he could.

This was a whole new experience for me as although the children that shared our home usually arrived with various levels of hygiene and different levels of understanding, they would normally be very quiet and possibly a bit wary or... far more concerning...overly loving and affectionate.

I knew things would settle down...I just hoped it would be soon.

But Peter and Carl are another story...Suffice to say that they were part of our family for the following 18 months and will be fleetingly mentioned at some point further in Mia's story.

Who knows, maybe I will write their story one day in the future.

Chapter 18

It was when Mia was coming up to thirteen months and had been a part of our family for just over seven months of her life that it was felt Mia should have a more substantial car seat.

One weekend, as Carl and Peter were spending time with their grandparents, Howard and I decided to visit some friends who lived about a hundred miles from our home.

Because of the distance and Mia's disabilities we rarely managed to see them but this weekend was special as it was around three of our birthdays.

Howard and I packed everything we would need for the day and set off.

We couldn't risk going for overnight visits as Mia may need emergency support and to be so far from home and our local hospital where everyone knew her for an overnight stay was not a good idea...overnight being when Mia seemed to have her most appalling seizures.

We were within about half a mile from our friends home when, as we went around a round-about, Mia had a major epileptic fit and somehow managed to almost come out of her car seat.

Howard, sitting in the front passenger seat managed to support her as he climbed into the back of the car while I drove to a safe area to pull off the road.

Howard then sat cradling Mia until we got to our friends home.

Fortunately, though it was quite a big fit, Mia seemed to come out of it okay and we spent a relaxing day with our friends in their garden.

Howard sat in the back all the way home in case Mia had another seizure during the journey.

It was after this that we pursued the purchase of a more secure seat for Mia, finally getting one that had a seven point harness; over her shoulders and across her chest; her abdomen and between her legs.

Unfortunately it would be a little while before we could say that Mia was totally safe when went out in the car because the seat she had was the right one for our car even if it wasn't the right one for her…in fact, it was only when we purchased a new car that things progressed on this front as, regardless of what funding was available to the department of social services…they have a duty to keep children safe…they had no option but to provide car seats that fitted our new car. But I had learned a valuable lesson that day…one eye on the road and what was going on outside of the car…and one eye on Mia and what was happening for her inside the car.

We also now heard that Mia's dad had been to court and been bailed pending a sentencing date later in the year. He had been charged with GBH.

Chapter 19

All children in the care system have review meetings where information is shared about how things are for them and plans are made regarding their future.

The time for Mia's second review since moving in with us had arrived. When Mia's first review had been held her father had been unable to attend. Now he had been bailed and expected to be party to all information shared first hand. Due to the situation between her birth parents it was decided that two reviews would be held, one for each parent with the same information and future plans being shared and given.

It was decided to continue with the Care Plan as it stood, however, although Mia's father was happy for things to continue as they were the mother was not happy with this as she wanted Mia to be returned to her care.

Because Mia was now eating three meals a day, even lumpy food was being thoroughly enjoyed, and fortunately with a preference for savoury meals or she may have gained even more weight...and she had managed to sit unsupported for about a minute recently, which was a small act that had brought tears of joy to our eyes, the mother didn't appear to appreciate how poorly Mia was and certainly didn't appear to understand the enormity of this simple action.

It was as if the mother thought because Mia had sat...she must be getting better...

I was lucky to have so many people working for Mia that supported her remaining with our family at the meeting. One by one they gave their reasons for her remaining where she was. The physiotherapist explained that Mia needs to be settled when having her therapy and she now visited Mia at home as she got more out of each session this way. Everyone's reasons appeared to be centred on Mia being settled where she was.

Everyone was pleased with Mia's progress but acknowledged that both short and long term needs for specialist equipment had to be considered and that she would need long term intervention by all agencies currently working with her.

Fortunately the professionals at the review were aware of Mia's very complex needs and though she was starting to thrive in many areas, she was still a very poorly baby with nine outside agencies helping me to care for her. This meant a tremendous amount of time had to be given to attending appointments not only in our local area but also in London and everyone knew that we were not only managing that very well but also committed to doing everything in our power to ensure Mia had as good a quality of life as was humanly possible...for as long as that may be.

Of course, with the best will in the world and everyone wanting Mia to remain where she was, there are guidelines that have to be followed. The mother wanted to have a parenting assessment to show she was capable of looking after Mia better than anyone else could and the department had to agree to this.

The reviewing officer explained to the mother parallel planning was underway. This is where two plans are followed…one for return to birth family and one for long term care though fostering or on to adoption, depending on the case being worked.

There was to be a home assessment for the mother, pending the outcome of a psychiatric report, which would be done over six weeks in her own home between the hours of 0900 and 1700 pending the outcome of an assessment of her capabilities to parent Mia appropriately.

Additional contact for both parents was at this time denied so as not to disrupt Mia's routine or infringe on her on-going appointments.

Now all we had to do was wait to see the outcome of the mother's psychiatric assessment and we would know in what direction we were travelling.

Chapter 20

The mother had been given my home phone number right at the start of this placement so she could phone once a week for an update on how Mia was getting on; what sort of day she'd had etc...

Two days after the review I received a phone call from the mother.

Initially she asked how Mia was and if it was okay for contact to go ahead the following day. I had forgotten about the change in contact days and had made arrangements to be somewhere else and said it would be in Mia's best interest to be with me as I was going to a university to see how they worked their sensory room. This was agreed to by the mother.

The mother then started to discuss the review decisions. Part of the discussion had been around respite care for Mia. Sharon was no longer readily available due to her other placements so I had visited another carer with a view to her providing this valuable support. I was not aware that the social worker had discussed that visit with the mother in any detail and was surprised when she told me she knew the visit had been unsatisfactory due to the house being filthy and us not being allowed to see

71

the kitchen...she also asked me if I could 'pull any strings' and get things moving on, even if it meant finding someone and checking them out myself. I had to explain to her the thorough vetting system that prospective carers go through, explaining that to be approved takes many months of training and interviews, then attending a panel for the final decision to be made, so no, I could not pull any strings or just find 'someone' to stand in during an emergency.

The mother then started to discuss her home assessment. She asked me if I could write down what Mia's different screams sound like and the reasons for her screaming. I told her that would be impossible...how do you describe a sound in writing? I did however tell her that the screaming could be for any number of reasons such as pain, boredom, hunger, thirst or frustration and was surprised by her response that if Mia's brain was so badly damaged, how would she know if she was bored or in pain.

By now the mother had gone into complaining mode... Why could I have people in the house during the day and she can't for the duration of the assessment. It didn't seem to register with her that not only did I have three children under school age all with special needs of their own and therefore needing the extra support afforded me by the department, but that I wasn't the one being assessed either.

And of course...she felt that the department were setting her up to fail and couldn't appear to comprehend that if she failed it was because she was unable to manage everything involved with caring for Mia entailed.

The mother then totally stumped me when she said "I've heard from one or two people that the assessment can be held at your house but you've said no".

I could not believe what she had said…did she really think I would allow her through my front door? I didn't want her to put one foot on my drive let alone come into our home!

I told her that I hadn't been approached and if I were to be…I would refuse.

No point in saying anything different really as to do so may leave the door open for her to approach the department and ask if she could be assessed here…with me on hand to help and advise her. No…she wanted the assessment so I would give her all the necessary information needed to ensure Mia had as easy a time as possible, but I could not sit and physically watch this woman trying to care for the child I had come to love so very much.

****

Our daughter Claire had managed through a friend of hers at university, to book as long a session as we wanted in the sensory room as the university was all but closed for the holidays. I hadn't told the mother it was an unofficial visit organized by Claire as I felt she may have caused a problem, but I had made the social workers aware of this.

The following day I drove with my daughter Claire and Mia to the university. Fortunately, although it was a good few miles drive away Mia's epilepsy seemed quite well controlled for the drive. We arrived at the near deserted campus in an absolute downpour and parked as close to the building as possible, then we ran, with Mia in my arms into the building.

When we entered the sensory department, I was amazed at what I saw.

The equipment they had was like nothing I had ever seen before and they were letting me use it to assess if Mia would benefit from any of the activities she could do here.

A huge area of the floor was covered in soft mats for floor exercise, there was a massive cloth swing that she snuggled into and the audio room was amazing. There were so many things to look at and for Mia to try but the best thing of all was the bubble light tube. Mia's response to this was huge (as was the bubble light tube) and refocused me on completing her sensory area at home. I wasn't sure if it was the lights or the vibration of the tube or both so we decided we would get the biggest tube we could find that would go into our home and fit in her sensory corner.

Mia also had a very good response to the mirror light ball. Again, this was a large ball and a powerful light so we went in search of a similar one for our home which we could use in any area…We mostly used this, once we had purchased it, in Mia's bedroom, calling the dancing light's 'Mia's fairies' as they calmed her so much.

Chapter 21

When Mia was fourteen months I took her to see one of her many specialist doctors for a check-up.

Once again her disabilities were pointed out in black and white to me;

Previous non-accidental head injury.

Consequent to this current functional problems are:

Global developmental delay

Epilepsy (recently control of epilepsy has become poor with increasing number of absences and tonic fits). Anticonvulsant added today.

Severe visual impairment.

Microcephaly (small head)

Constipation

Motor impairment – mixture of hypertonia or spasticity. Her head control is poor with weak neck extensions and is still unable to sit without support. Her back is slightly curved when lifted under the armpit she appears to be floppy.

Regarding Mia's epilepsy the doctor had no choice but to increase her anticonvulsant medications as she'd had a brief tonic fit which had lasted about forty seconds the previous evening while in the bath…and he found examining her difficult as she appeared to be having quite a few little absences while we were with him. We would keep in touch and I would let him know of any side effects to the new regime.

He noted that Mia could coo when she was happy and that she turned her head towards me when I spoke. It was also noted that she appeared able to see bright lights so would possibly know the difference between light and dark…something most of us take for granted.

One thing that the doctor pointed out and was something that I hadn't really thought of, Mia didn't bring her hands to the bottle when having a feed.

This is what happens when you care for a profoundly disabled child…you do everything you can to keep them safe and content and so focused on the milestones they reach that you don't always realise some milestones are being passed and not reached.

You react with such total joy and excitement at every little thing they manage to achieve and somehow, while celebrating these huge victories…don't notice that some things are just not happening.

The doctor then assessed Mia's development using the Schedule of Growing Skills 2 (developmental assessment for children between 0-5 years)

Passive postural skills	3 months
Active postural skills	1 month

Manipulative skills	3 months
Visual skills unable to assess due to fitting	
Hearing and Language skills	12 months
Speech and language skills	3 months
Interactive social skills	3 months
Self-care social skills	0-6 months

The report went on to say that Mia showed significant developmental delay due to her non-accidental head injury and her hearing and language skills appear to be fairly age appropriate because her hearing was fairly intact. He noted that the areas of developmental delay were due to the combined impact of her visual impairment together with her motor impairment and cognitive impairment.

We did however leave with a few of positives…Mia's heart, chest and abdomen were normal.

Two days later she was rushed to hospital after having a major epileptic fit which meant she had to remain there for two days while her medication was once again 'tweaked'.

Chapter 22

My personal feelings toward the mother remained quite mixed. Sometimes the mother was quite pleasant towards me and appeared to respond well to Mia; but it was Mia I watched at these times and she would usually become distressed whenever the mother was near which was concerning. Mia would actually tense up and whimper as soon as she heard the mother's voice when she had attended appointments with us and I had arrived before her and was already sitting in the waiting room. Poor Mia, she did her best to let us know how she felt even without the ability to verbalize.

Unfortunately though, Mia had now started to have more fits.

One morning when we went into the nursery we saw evidence that she'd had such a big fit sometime between us checking her before going to bed and waking in the morning, that by the time I got to her she had a large friction burn on her face.

It had been such a quiet night.

A night where both Howard and I slept soundly as did the children.

Then the morning arrived and with it...oh boy...poor Mia...

Howard had gone in to check Mia while I made us our first cup of coffee.

Howard was clearly quite shocked and upset, calling me straight away to check Mia with him.

Mia was lying across her cot. At that time she was just coming out of a fit. But she was so quiet. Usually there was some sound, something that would alert us, even if it was just the sound of the bedding and her soft toys moving. Her head was just twitching a little bit; but her face was against a soft cuddly toy.

She had what appeared to be a friction burn over her forehead, left cheek, and eyelid.

I checked the cot to see what could cause such damage.

There were only soft fabrics in Mia's cot. We only ever used soft fabrics because Mia had such delicate skin.

As Mia settled I continued to check her bedding.

Then I found it...the offending item was a soft toy!

Mia had produced a small amount of vomit which had gone onto one of the soft toys she had in the cot with her. This had made the soft fur go hard and become abrasive.

Another hazard had been identified and we would have to consider very carefully what was in Mia's cot in the future. This would have to include the bedding used as some baby blankets are beautiful and soft but when vomit hits them they also become abrasive and hard and can cause horrendous injuries if anyone should be in a position of continuous involuntary movement such as when having an epileptic episode. I moved all her soft toys to the bottom of the cot so she could just feel them with her feet.

Following this incident Howard and I were interviewed by the manager of the Children with Disabilities team. These interviews, although procedural and quite right to ensure the carers haven't done anything to cause the injury to the child they are looking after, still causes the carers dismay to a certain degree. This interview was important not only to ensure we were caring for Mia properly, but also to ensure that the department had all the relevant information regarding what had happened so they could answer any allegations made by the mother about us now or in the near future.

Right then though I had to sooth Mia's face and make a telephone call to Doctor Frankie for advice.

Chapter 23

Mia had remained calm and settled until I took her to see Doctor Frankie after her morning clinic.

Doctor Frankie was aware that Mia's fits had become worse over the past week and, where Mia had been having only small minor fits with absences and generalised brief loss of consciousness, now there was also the associated tonic movements involving her arms with her head moving to one side.

Mia's medication dosages were changed and another anticonvulsant added.

Doctor Frankie also noted that Mia didn't look at all well and noted that she had a few minor fits while we were there.

We then went on to the hospital to get the injury photographed and recorded as everyone knew that the mother would accuse me of abusing Mia...we'd already been down that road when, one morning while everything was nice and peaceful, I had laid Mia on the settee.

As Mia had a tendency to roll her hips and head to the right, I no longer laid her with her head towards the door end of the settee, which meant she could actually roll off and fall to the floor, but with her head towards the end where we had a small wall unit.

I knew she couldn't fall and Peter and Carl were playing on the floor. Mia was just lying peacefully, as usual so was quite safe.

Peter was now coming up to a year old and Carl was nearly four.

Carl, as usual was playing nicely with some cars, lying on the floor with the little road mat he liked to use.

I was standing just in the doorway to the playroom when Carl suddenly jumped up from the floor; he had seen something he wanted and quick as a flash he climbed onto the settee and reached for a toy that was on the unit next to where Mia was lying.

Mia started to cry as Carl's knee came into contact with her head. Carl started to cry because Mia was crying...Peter fortunately ignored everyone and carried on chewing on a toy.

I quickly checked that Mia was okay, picking her up and comforting her, while trying to comfort Carl as well and reassure him that I wasn't cross with him. Mia settled down, as did Carl who went back to playing with the toys.

About twenty minutes later when one of the contact support workers arrived to take Mia to see her mother, Mia threw up.

Not the whole feed she'd had earlier, and she didn't need changing.

But sick enough to cause concern due to the knock she'd had to her head.

I explained to the support worker that Mia had had a bump to the head, but also that there was a virus going round, so perhaps that was the reason for the sickness. Also, historically, Mia was a sickly baby after feeds.

The contact worker checked Mia over and as she was quite calm and peaceful decided that contact with the mother should go ahead so off she and Mia went to see the mother.

Not long after that I had a telephone call to say Mia had been violently sick, so it had been suggested she be taken to hospital, just in case it was anything to do with the bump.

Shit...Mia didn't need this.

She didn't need another head injury.

I didn't need another complaint from the mother going in to the office either.

Fortunately after a hurried telephone conversation Elizabeth very quickly came to babysit and I hurried over to the hospital.

When I got to the ward not only was a social worker there, but the mother was there as well.

The first angry words out of the mother's mouth were "who hit Mia on the head?"

I told her Mia had not been hit, she had in fact been bumped, and it was not a deliberate act, but an accident involving a very gentle child.

I then went over events of the morning with her, the social worker and the doctor, then after some x rays, it was decided to keep Mia in for 24 hours observation. I hated leaving her in the hospital, but had to get home to the other children and allow Elizabeth to get home to care for her family.

We had a restless night at home and just hoped that no extra damage had occurred and that Mia would be home the next day.

The following day with a feeling of total relief I bought Mia home. This was as much to the relief of family and friends as it was to Howard and I.

A few days later Mia came home from contact with a couple of nasty scratches on her leg. Fortunately I saw them before the contact social worker left so she logged them as well.

By this time any semblance of a relationship I had with Mia's mother was out of the window.

Truth be known, I suppose it went out the window from day one because, no matter what the mother felt at that first meeting towards me...I felt nothing but disgust for them.

Not disgust because they had injured this child because I didn't know if they had. Simply disgusted that the help this child had needed was not immediately sought out.

I had subsequently been informed that the mother hadn't considered Mia's injury as important enough to immediately warrant a telephone call to get an ambulance to the scene right away. (This was borne out some months later in an article about Mia in the local papers, when her father was sentenced to two-and-a-half-years imprisonment for causing the damage to her). In fact, it appears that the mother went shopping to several different shops gathering timed receipts to evidence she hadn't been around at the time of the injury...and then, when the emergency services were called, only asked for a paramedic to attend...who immediately called for ambulance support as they clearly saw how badly Mia was injured. The police were also informed and arrived at the parent's home to question them about what had happened.

At this point Mia was unconscious and non-reactive, she had bruises above her eyes and was having fits. When she arrived at the hospital Mia had to be resuscitated...Mia's father had then been arrested at the hospital on suspicion of manslaughter as it was felt Mia was going to die.

Because the hospital had managed to successfully resuscitated Mia, instead of arresting her, the mother was permitted to travel with Mia to Great Ormond Street Hospital as permission was need for any operation that may be considered necessary.

The mother then delayed Mia being taken to Great Ormond Street Hospital as she needed to return to her home to collect some items for herself...I just couldn't get my head around the knowledge that if that had been my child or a friends child or almost any member of the general public's child...a responsible adult would have called for an ambulance and sod what we needed from home...we would be off to wherever in the country we needed to go to get the best support for an injured baby.

If I didn't have to behave in a professional way when around the mother I don't know what I would have said...though went through quite a few different scenarios.

Oh how I loved my private little conversations held within my head, between me and the mother...oh to be free to tell her what an utter dirt bag I considered her to be...and of course quite a few stronger words would invariably be thrown in.

Oh yes...in my private conversations within my head...the mother knew exactly what I thought of her and the father.

Chapter 24

Around this time we had brought a new car and I had to get new car seats for the children. This made sense as we all need to be safe when out and about.

Meeting the needs of Peter and Carl was no problem. I quickly had seats sorted not only for their body size and ages, but also the right seats for our car.

Now, finding a car seat for Mia, who was unfortunately, at this time having quite a few epileptic episodes proved problematic. Though none of her epileptic episodes lasted a long time, they were bad in that Mia's arms would both rise up, her back would become arched and her eyes would roll.

So there we were, having succeeded with Peter and Carls car seats, waiting for a suitable seat to be organised for Mia.

I picked one out that I liked. It looked expensive…it probably was expensive, but I didn't care as I only wanted the best for 'my' children…and I wasn't picking up the bill as social services supplied the vital equipment needed for us to do our job.

The man who had the job of making sure the seat was right all round looked at me.

He then looked at Mia, who was now having a fit.

He looked back at me and took several other baby seats from the shelf and we went back to the car.

I was so chuffed when the seat I had chosen was considered a good fit for my motor...but, the man did not consider it as safe for Mia, because not only should Mia (in his opinion, having seen her have a fit) be in a rear facing seat as he felt she needed it to be reclined, he also felt she needed a more secure body harness to make sure she didn't come out of the seat if she had a major epileptic episode while we were driving along. There was also the problem of Mia needing extra support just to sit in a car seat, even if reclined as she was like a new born baby with no way to support her own body weight.

Now, for Mia to be in a rear facing seat, she had to be in the front of the car with me so I could keep an eye on her.

Unfortunately sitting in the front was not really an option as we had airbags which could not easily be de-activated.

If we could get a good front facing seat, with enough support, she could sit behind me.

I would have to speak with Sarah later to find out where the department were with ordering her a specialised car seat with the right amount of support and straps to ensure her safety when we were out driving.

Of course, with the purchase of the new car came a series of questions from the mother...was it new; did it have air bags; did we have air con...

I felt like saying it was the oldest rustiest old banger we could find with no mod cons and what the hell is air con?

But of course, I bit my tongue; smiled and gave the right answers.

Our new motor was then deemed suitable to transport Mia in by the mother, though she had made no mention of what the car seat was like or if it had been professionally fitted.

I was lucky this time as within a couple of weeks Mia and I were to visit the wheelchair clinic and order not only her fantastic car seat which would make all the difference to keeping her safe, but also her wheelchair as she no longer had the right amount of support from the pushchair I used…the only downside to her wheelchair was that it didn't have the same amount of suspension so every time it wheeled over something or you went up and down the kerb the ride wasn't so smooth for Mia.

****

Finally the day arrived, after what seemed like an eternity, (though in reality it was only a few weeks) for us to visit the little cottage hospital in the next town to have Mia fitted for a car seat.

I was so very pleased with what they sorted for her.

Mia sat beautifully in it and looked totally safe and contented. This seat, though quite large and cumbersome, had a seven point harness.

No chance of her ever having a fit and falling out of this one.

We also had the fitting for Mia to have a wheelchair for when it was just her going out.

Even baby wheelchairs are heavy and cumbersome.

She was not considered a suitable candidate for one of the 'buggy' type chairs so we had a heavy set of wheels ordered; no suspension on these things, but they did lay back and come with all mod cons,like a brake and a hood for in the wet weather.

We actually had a really good morning all round, even Mia's fits were fewer than of late.

Again I had to ask the mother via the contact book to give Mia some back physiotherapy. I even wrote that this was the most important thing for Mia at the moment as she had so much mucus to shift and was really quite rattley at that time.

A deaf person can hear Mia rattle you selfish bastard...do something for her will you!

Again I asked the mother to use the swabs and told her that sometimes Mia can use a dozen or more a day

One got used during contact as the mother said Mia "chewed" on them...didn't they realise this was possibly because Mia was thirsty or had a dry mouth and wanted more moisture?

The mother's only response was to let me know that she thought Mia was more alert than usual.

Chapter 25

The messages I was now getting back through the contact book could be quite abrupt.

Mia was still back to using swabs and I had to ask repeatedly that they be used.

Complaints were coming back after every contact that Mia had been sick; she'd had a dirty nappy when she arrived (these, when the mother changed them were put back into the baby bag in a plastic sack instead of being disposed of in the bins at the contact suite); complaints that the contact bag had faeces in (who put's soiled nappies in the bag? Not me).

On one occasion there was a message asking me to change a soiled nappy on Mia's return...the mother had refused to change it as they decided for that day that they would not be involved in the personal care of Mia until she was returned to them.

I was also using the communication book to ask permission for Mia to have her vaccinations, as I needed evidence that the mother had consented and they refused to write a letter of consent to anyone.

Even when a child is in care, the parents need to consent to vaccinations being done until they no longer have parental control of the child as directed by the court.

Consent was never given and Mia didn't get any protection from normal childhood illnesses; which left her extremely vulnerable and meant we had to be extra vigilant when we were out with her.

It got to the stage where whoever bought Mia home from contact had to wait while I read the content of what had been written before leaving. If there was a comment that Mia was sore I had the contact staff check the area to see if there was in fact any soreness, and then wrote to the mother that Mia had been checked by a social worker on returning home and that there were no issues.

Demands would then be made by the mothers for information on which social worker had checked Mia.

Chapter 26

The mother would still phone once a week for an update on how Mia was getting on; what sort of day she'd had etc...

Tonight the mother phoned.

The mother could only phone on a none contact day as it was a waste of time to phone when she had seen Mia earlier in the day, as we had a contact book up and running between us so the mother had all the news three times a week anyway...and it wasn't as if I would ever write to let her know Mia had taken her first step was it...not after what she'd gone through, possibly at the hands of the mother.

Oh no...I was never going to say Mia was singing; laughing; dancing for joy...was I.

So there's the mother on the phone moaning about everything and everybody.

The mother started complaining about when Mia's head had got a bump from Carl climbing up for his toy and let me know she had taken photos of it.

I asked the mother if they ever took any nice photos of Mia, as all she ever seemed to do was take photos of marks, real or imagined.

The mother said she had taken lots of nice photos, but now needed photos of any bruising as evidence that Mia was being abused while in care and by me, and the mother could show these pictures to a judge and tell this judge that she, the mother, could guarantee this would not have happened if Mia had been in her care.

Bugger me backwards...if only Mia had received a small bruise...a huge bruise even...at the hands of the mother...at least she would perhaps have more than just an existence, at least then she would maybe, just maybe, have had the chance of growing up to do all the things normal healthy little girls do.

The things this once normal and healthy little girl had been born to do.

And here the mother was...guaranteeing that Mia wouldn't get a bruise if in her care.

Thanks to another phone call from the mother I now knew she had delayed calling for help in case the social services took her other children from her as well as Mia...something which had subsequently happened as they now lived with their birth father and when I had met him and seen the children for a contact visit in our home I thought how much more relaxed and settled they seemed...and what a nice man their father was.

I diversify a little here but I think it's important to know that I had met the mother's children a few times when I had taken Mia to contact and had always found the eldest to be a bit surly...but here he was, with his younger sibling, father and paternal grandmother, who was also one of the nicest people I had met, relaxed and chatty in my home. There was such a transformation in the time the children had moved to their fathers I was totally amazed...and obviously very pleased for the children.

I wanted to shout into that smug face of hers "You total bastard! How dare you think you can make such stupid promises; guaranties; after what you did!"

But of course, I didn't.

Protocol wouldn't allow for that...and besides, I didn't know what she had done...I only thought her responsible and fully accepted that my opinions could be flawed due to the feelings I had for Mia.

And anyway, what would be the point...the mother appeared to have no shame and appeared also to feel no guilt.

They were the ones being hurt weren't they?

They were the ones being denied a normal life with their child weren't they?

Funny, but now, according to the mother, it was the fault of social services and my family that Mia wasn't living with her at her home.

What transference of blame the mother could work. How easily she had sat back and re-written history. This was truly laughable if it wasn't so bloody tragic.

I asked the mother if she wanted Mia moved to another carer and the answer given was a definite no.

Lying bitch!

I asked the mother why she was trying to build a case against me if she didn't want Mia moved.

The mother said she wasn't building a case against me, just one against social services.

Double lying bitch!

I then, rather foolishly and totally unprofessionally, asked the mother if she was stupid or what, and that, just suppose she did show these pictures to a judge, and just suppose the judge did agree with whatever the mother was saying, did she then expect this judge to say, "yeah, fine, Mia is being abused, but we'll leave her where she is anyway."

Bloody hell, this mother was a total frigging nutter who seemed to do anything to get attention...only thing is this mother went after any attention, even negatives.

Any attention seemed better than none for her. But we wanted a peaceful life for our family and a peaceful life for Mia. We didn't want anyone rocking our boat...Mia's boat...

Though Howard and I were fairly secure in our opinion of ourselves as people, and the departments opinion of us as a family, we were still terrified that the mother may just manage to stir up enough unrest with all the lies that she told the department and that they would decide to move forward with adoption for Mia...and no-one in our family could bear the thought of Mia living with another family.

Hell, no other family could care for Mia like we do.

No other family would ever love her like we do.

My mind was wandering...pondering different outcomes for Mia...

The mother was prattling on and I was still only half listening to her because apart from my mind wandering, there was something interesting on the television and there is only so much self-pitying whining you can take at the end of a busy day, when the mother said

"I've got contacts in social services, and they tell me things."

I tried to concentrate and listen a bit better then, even though I knew this was probably another lie and just said to cause me concern.

The mother then rattled on about lots of different things, one of them being that when they repeated things, they sometimes twisted these things a little bit (like I hadn't worked that one out for myself already...stupid bastard!) as she liked to tell people what they wanted to hear, which may not always be the whole truth.

Fortunately a few social workers involved in this case had brains and had also worked that one out, as stories had abounded regarding social workers as well.

The mother also asked me where I got the information about her leaving Mia for over 3 hours before getting help, because the mother claimed now, she had only left her for 1 hour.

Oh...that's okay then.

Mia is badly injured.

She is limp.

She is not responding.

She has what looks to be two black eyes.

She is having fits…

And for you, you bastard to leave her for; for even a second is beyond unforgivable!

How dare you try to justify yourself! I'm living every minute of every day with a child whose life you have ruined! A child whose life you have stolen away from her.

Because you have stolen it away as surely as if you had physically done the damage to her…(something I still consider she did even though the father admitted to it…he was just a kid and the mother was a manipulative older woman).

I hate you! I hate you! I hate you!

Go rot in hell where you belong you totally evil scumbag!

Such a pity I can't say what I want to say.

I wander how many cigarettes the mother had; how many cups of tea they drank, while Mia lay there.

Did the mother hold her; did she speak to her…

No.

I already knew the mother didn't do that.

The mother didn't seem capable of having feelings for anyone but herself.

From what the mother had told me about her childhood my feelings were that she suffered from emotional deprivation from a very young age, growing up in a family where all the attention was directed at her younger and brainier sibling and now, as an adult she just didn't know how to care for anyone other than herself, which was sad…but couldn't be used as an excuse for her total lack of empathy for Mia when she had needed a mother to protect her.

The mother went a bit quiet when I told her that it was herself that had told me. I reminded her of the times we had spent talking when she had chosen to attend the ophthalmology clinic or any of the other appointments with me and Mia. The mother had always liked to talk, especially when she spoke about her hatred for her ex-husband and his new family or herself and what she wanted. Especially when she wanted people to know how she had been abused by the 'system'. The mother never spoke of her concern for Mia during these times it was all self; self; self.

It was a very uncomfortable call and I'd ended up saying I had to go, though did tell the mother first that she had better make sure that when she reported this conversation, she did so accurately, as I certainly would be.

The mother never made any more calls like that one and, to my knowledge, didn't show the photos she had taken to any judge.

Not that that would have been a problem…social services and the medical profession had some pretty good negatives themselves for a judge to look at, albeit of Mia's injuries and I had some wonderful photos of her within my family, looking just beautiful.

Chapter 27

When caring for anyone with disabilities you encounter many different hazards.

We already knew Mia couldn't get out of the way of the other children that lived with us as they played on the floor or our granddaughters when they came to play.

We knew we had to make sure there was no hard or sharp objects near Mia; though that was taken care of anyway as we had the other children to consider...general common sense made sure sharp objects were kept in a secure place.

We were also aware that we had to be almost over protective of Mia when mixing with other children, in part due to her complex needs and partly because the mother had refused to give her written consent in case Mia suffered 'brain damage' from having them she had been denied the opportunity of having any vaccinations against the normal childhood illnesses.

One hazard though that we hadn't considered, was the sun and now summer was fast approaching we were going to learn a few lessons and fast.

I hadn't thought the sun would be a problem as we used sun creams on the children and they had hats if it was particularly hot outside.

One problem facing people who have a disability is that they are usually on various medications and sometimes, quite a toxic cocktail of medication at that.

Medications not only heal, they can also affect the way your body acts when exposed to the elements.

Mia could be in her pram on a lovely warm day, with the sun peeping out from behind the clouds...

And burn.

Mia could get a nasty sun burn even walking to the shops with the canopy shading her as she lay in the pram.

Mia could also turn blue in hot weather because her circulation was so bad.

A pet hate for me is the cold.

I do not cope with the cold very well at all and will find myself, even in the summer evenings when it is warm to everyone else, slipping into a jumper and fluffy socks; so to see Mia's little feet turn blue and feel so chilled even on a hot day, where she could get a sunburned face was awful.

There were still so many things to learn about Mia, even though she had shared our home and our hearts for some time now.

Chapter 28

Just as summer peeped round the corner Mia had a huge epileptic fit which saw her back in hospital…this time she had to stay for two weeks because of difficulties with her feeding and uncontrolled fitting. During the time Mia was in hospital she was put back onto tube feeds and all her medications were adjusted, with a new one added.

Peter and Carl had two weeks of topsy-turvy living as I juggled spending quality time with them and quality time with Mia.

Even super mum couldn't do that and I'm no-where near being a super mum, being content with just being me, a happy mum for most of the time.

Everyone lost out in one way or another.

Poor Howard was coming home from a hard day in the office and taking over the job of getting the boys to bed and then cooking his own meal while I said hello and goodbye as I ran out of the front door to spend time with Mia.

We were like ships that passed in the night.

Our longest conversations were over the telephone wires and mostly consisted of instructions from me to him or vice versa concerning Peter and Carl.

It was only as we fell exhausted into bed at the end of each day that we would speak of Mia...of our concerns...Howard comforted me and reassured me that she would be fine, though I knew he had the same fears as I did.

What if this time she isn't?

All anyone could do now was to wait.

Wait and pray.

And then there was more upset for us, as we had booked to go away with friends for two weeks.

The last thing Howard and I wanted was to not be here for Mia when she came out of hospital...but sods law...Mia was allowed home the day before we were leaving and went straight to stay with Sharon and her family, this being done in order to cause her minimum disruption. This was to cause as little distress as possible to her. I understood this and accepted it as the best at the time, but oh how we had wanted her to come home to us because we also knew Mia would be unsettled for a few days at least as we were not with her.

All the arrangements had been made months ago for Mia to stay with Sharon and her family while we were away. It made sense as Mia knew Sharon and appeared settled in her home. Also, Sharon was well used to sorting out medication so everything Mia would need was packed up and delivered to Sharon's home.

It just wasn't viable for Mia to come home for one night and then be moved.

It wasn't right either for us to let our friends down by cancelling our holiday, though they would have understood...the department of social services wouldn't and I knew my link worker would not be amused if we had cancelled our holiday after the year we had just been through.

So we went away with our friends. We flew to Turkey and lazed in the sun. We spent our time reading books; sightseeing and enjoying our friends company.

We found time to enjoy each other's company with no distractions and we would come home with our batteries recharged and ready for whatever Mia and the world might throw our way. Ready to face the mother and whatever she had planned to make our lives as miserable as she could.

Being on holiday also meant I missed a Multi-disciplinary assessment which advised Sharon to try Mia on some baby rice to see if she could tolerate it.

I know it sounds quite big headed but, I think they tried to move her on too quickly. Had they waited for us to return from our holiday before trying Mia with solids again she may have been more relaxed and taken them...or maybe I would have asked them not to even try just yet due to how poorly she still was, but by the time we got home and Mia joined our family again she was totally tube fed.

An urgent referral was made for the following month for Mia to attend great Ormond Street hospital for investigation into her feeding difficulties…this was then cancelled with a new appointment made for three months later.

Mia remained, for now quite unstable with no two days being the same as far as feeding, sickness and her epilepsy were concerned and she was introduced to another epilepsy medication…she was now on four anticonvulsant medicines as well as one anti sickness and two laxative medications.

One of Mia's new medicines was called Ethosuximide. This seemed to work well with a noticeable reduction in Mia's rapid eye movement which made it easier to detect, monitor and manage her fits. Mia also appeared to be more alert and relaxed which was another bonus.

There was also a standing frame delivered for Mia to use a couple of times a day. Mia seemed to enjoy her time strapped into the frame and it was hoped that by having another position to be in her sickness may improve a little and more feeds would be kept down. We were, at this time having to give all medication at least an hour before feeds as she was still being so very sick that there were concerns she was not getting the full benefit of the medications she was on.

Mia was still having back massage before every meal and her medications to shift any mucus build up that may have been making her throw back everything that went down her feeding tube.

Chapter 29

When we returned two weeks later it was to a whole new feeding and medicating regime to get used to.

Mia was now on six feeds a day starting at 0600 and ending around 21:00.

Welcome home mummy and daddy. There would be no more sleeping in now.

With Mia being tube fed, she could sleep as peacefully as she wanted...she would get fed irrespective of if she was awake or not.

The only reason she would have a delayed feed was if she was having a seizure because when Mia had a seizure...everything stopped.

Peter and Carl arrived home the day after we bought Mia home, giving us time to settle in and get some laundry done.

Thank goodness their grandmother being the lovely kind and considerate person she was, had done all their laundry so all we had to do was put everything away.

Soon everyone seemed to have settled back in okay.

So life continued...

Mia had good nights where she would sleep so peacefully that I would get up to make sure she was okay...Funny how the silence can wake you.

And bad nights when I would sit with her and reassure her she was not alone as she had a flurry of little fits that though concerning, didn't warrant calling an ambulance out and disrupting the whole household.

In many ways Mia seemed to improve over the following few days, becoming very active and quite vocal.

Her feeds stayed down, which was good, but she started to be a bit sick after her medication in the mornings.

We had been home just over a week, following the regime of feeds and medication which had been changed while we were away.

Mia seemed to be finding it too much having six feeds a day. It seemed like she had just settled down from one feed when it was time to start feeding her again. Also, Mia kept being sick on this new formula she had been given.

Mia was becoming so distressed with the amount of feds she was having and the number of times she was being sick that I telephoned the dietician and she agreed to reduce the amount of feeds to five lots of 140mls.

That was good.

Now Mia would only throw back five feeds of Neocate Advance, the special formula she was now taking instead of the normal baby formula.

Pity they didn't have a better formula for her.

Mia also had to have 400mls of water spread throughout the day. Some of this would be used to flush the tube before and after feeds the rest just as and when we could without making Mia sick.

We were given one little bonus for Mia though...we could now give Mia up to 5 teaspoons of solids once or twice a day.

Maybe...just maybe...we would take some bloody great big giant steps forward.

Chapter 30

Some days Mia was now having about fifteen fits in the morning alone. They would come in clusters…one after the other.

They weren't always very big but could last for between 1 and 2 minutes each.

One day started off so badly. Mia had been having these cluster fits that kept coming one after the other.

They were small, but persistent bloody fits.

Having taken medical advice and managing to get Mia back onto bottle feeds and solids she now barely managed to eat her lunch even with a lot of coaxing and was quite distressed.

Mia wanted her bottle but had difficulty latching on. She kept on having small fits which meant she kept letting go of the teat…so frustrating for both of us.

On this particular day though, Mia seemed to calm as the day wore on, and I wished, oh how I wished, that I'd had the camera rolling when we did the physiotherapy, as she was rubbing her hands together, (with my help), and touching her face and mouth.

Mia was just so relaxed, it was fantastic.

But the fits persisted and because of this Mia needed constant and close monitoring.

Sometimes now, though it has to be noted it is with a heavy heart, when Mia went to see her mother she took her feed with her. I hated to let the mother give Mia her meal because I knew Mia would not take it as easily as when she was at home and relaxed.

Mia still didn't relax or take her meals easily at these contact sessions and then I'd have the mother complaining to me that Mia should be tube fed, or that I should feed her before she went out.

Seems we can't do right for doing wrong. If I'd fed Mia before contact I was then denying the mother the right to feed her...if I'd left it for the mother to feed her I was deliberately sabotaging contact because I knew Mia would not take a feed from her.

We had to do everything at Mia's pace though, so if she slept late in the morning, every feed was delayed.

The only thing we couldn't delay is giving Mia her medicine.

I would wake her for this, but if she fell straight back to sleep I couldn't just pour food down her throat.

Wonder if that's what the mother would do...or maybe, she would just bugger off out and leave Mia to starve.

She certainly wouldn't put herself out to care properly for Mia.

The mother is far too important to herself to give any real time to Mia.

One day I got a message back after contact that Mia had a cold.

How frustrating is the mother! Of course we got concerned if Mia appeared to catch a cold, you just never knew if it was going to turn into something more serious, but half a drip from a baby's nose didn't mean they had a cold. The mother would say anything to try to show us in a bad light and themselves in a good and caring light.

The mother did very little real caring for Mia during her visits, leaving the supervisors or her mother (Mia's grandmother) to do nappy or clothe changes while she popped out for a smoke so I knew what would probably happen when she was told that Mia needed to have physiotherapy on her back at least three times a day.

These sessions were held before each meal and time allowing, before she went to bed as well as some time mid-morning and mid-afternoon.

This had been explained to the mother on several occasions by the contact supervisors and I had also spoken to her and shown her what to do yet still she refused to do anything during the time she spent with Mia that would make her more comfortable.

Mia did not have a cold. She had a build-up of mucus and that selfish bastard was doing nothing to help move it.

But of course...she had fun accusing me of all sorts of neglect, after all, as far as she was concerned, I had allowed Mia to catch a cold.

Chapter 31

Time went on. Sometimes we had a brilliant day with Mia, where everything went to plan. Others were a total nightmare where everything seemed so futile.

Sometimes when the physiotherapists or Tom came out to visit we would have a very good session with Mia responding in a positive way. Then we had the meetings when Mia would either just sleep or be totally unresponsive to everyone and everything.

Sadly though, there was one consistent activity happening. Mia was still having what had now become her usual fits.

One day when I had Mia's team; Tom and the physiotherapists, come to our home for a meeting to discuss how Mia was getting on and what our next steps were to be, I was saddened by the information given to me.

Everyone had arrived and they all seemed pleased with Mia's progress to date.

Tom then spoke of the need to start thinking about which school Mia would be attending.

For God's sake I thought...she's merely a baby...not yet a toddler.

Tom, dear kind patient Tom, went on to explain to me that children with Mia's complex needs could start school from the age of two years.

I could almost feel panic setting in…

I won't be ready for her to go then though.

Tom went on to explain that with Mia at school she would get the extra stimulation that I couldn't give her at home; and I would have the support of a larger team as well as a few hours of respite on a daily basis during the school term.

Oh my goodness…

Do I look like I need respite?

I probably did. I knew I probably needed it as well.

It was quite exhausting at times looking after Mia with all her physical needs and also with the constant worry of something happening to her I knew I rarely had a complete night's sleep.

It was suggested I keep a video diary (again), which I knew I had to try harder to find the time to complete, as I could see the value of having one, (as I could last time it had been suggested).

It was just sometimes so damn hard to find the extra seconds, let alone hours, needed each day to complete everything some of Mia's team wanted done.

It was agreed that they would send me details of a smaller daily exercise routine to follow which would target specific areas of Mia's development, as opposed to trying to do everything all at once.

I'm sure they also thought, cut the programme and I may find time to do the diary.

Oh how I have wished so very often, that I had found the time to keep that diary.

Chapter 32

Later that day Mia went to see the mother.

When she came home there was a message in the contact book from the mother saying that there seemed to be bruises on both Mia's legs around her ankles, and stating that she had taken photos of the said bruises.

There was also a comment from the mother that Mia's teeth seemed quite brown.

What the hell was the matter with the mother?

Did she not realise the damage that had been done to Mia all those months ago in a fit of temper?

Nothing was working properly in Mia's little body.

Surely she realised...well, should have realised having seen Mia three times a week for bloody months now that when her legs seemed to be cold and mottled red and blue that this was possibly an indication of Mia's poor temperature control.

Surely the mother must have noticed during other contacts that Mia's poor little legs were usually quite mottled looking, as they were that day, regardless of the weather.

And even I, with no medical background, knew that the regime of medication that Mia was taking, could quite possibly be the cause of any tooth decay, as no amount of cleaning them would bring them up shiny and white.

And as Mia had never had a sweetie to eat or a bottle of juice left hanging from her mouth, that really only left the medication anyway.

Chapter 33

Unfortunately, after a very good start to Mia's placement with us, getting her off nasogastric feeds and on to bottles and solids, which she initially took very well, we had a major setback which necessitated a return to nasogastric feeds. This was a huge blow to everyone involved in Mia's care and a blow to my confidence as it reasserted how little anyone could really control what was happening to Mia's little body, and how much damage had been done to her.

Mia had begun to have difficulty with her feeds. Some days, she would manage perfectly well, others she would have difficulty latching onto the teat of the bottle and gagged on solids.

During the early part of the summer, Mia's fit became poorly managed. Mia had a large fit at 4am one day, meaning I had to call for an ambulance, as we are not allowed to carry out 'invasive' procedures, and Mia needed an anal medication inserted.

We went to hospital in the ambulance and though she was monitored at this time I was asked to cuddle her as this was more reassuring than if she were strapped down. I was told that if her fits got worse the ambulance would stop; I would need to lay Mia on the stretcher immediately and they would carry out CPR if needed.

This was the most terrifying ride of my life.

Due to Mia's condition we went on 'Blues'...lights flashing but no sirens and got to the hospital in record time. It was thought the sirens would exacerbate the fits and, as it was so early in the morning there was little traffic to alert and get them out of our way.

Mia was lucky that morning as the fits subsided and she was allowed home later the same day.

Sadly she was readmitted three days later to have her fits stabilised and sort out her feeds as she kept being sick.

This time Mia stayed in hospital for the next two weeks, her bed right next to the nurse's station. Another cause for concern as she hadn't been placed that close since she had lived with our family.

While Mia was in hospital Howard and I took the other children on holiday. This did two things...gave us a break from the concerns of Mia and the possibility of meeting the mother as I was entering or leaving the building when she had her contact, which may sound selfish, but was necessary for our sanity, and gave the boys our undivided attention for a couple of weeks, which they relished.

Chapter 34

Following our holiday we found Mia back on six feeds a day, and five teaspoons of solids, which she kept bringing back. After discussing this with the dietician Mia's feed was changed and the amount of feeds reduced to five, then, after a short period of her still being sick, another reduction to four feeds a day.

The solids were also stopped at this time as there were concerns about Mia choking if she had a fit during a feed. Mia continued to be sick on an almost daily basis, though not to the extent that she had been. Mostly she would only vomit up a small amount of liquid, though on occasion she would kindly give the whole feedback.

We were now waiting for Mia to be assessed for a gastrostomy. Not something we wanted for her, to be fed through a tube in her tummy, but if she had to be tube fed, this was better than through a tube up her nose and down her throat. At least the gastrostomy would stay in, unlike the nasal feeding tube which certainly didn't.

Mia continued to be seen by physiotherapist, and made progress in her flexibility, though still made no attempt to touch most things without assistance from other people.

Mia was also still being seen by occupational therapist, and using her standing frame, something we would strap her into, that took all her weight and allowed her to 'feel her feet' which not only gave her another position apart from flat on her back or slightly raised but was also excellent in helping to prevent her being sick.

Mia would go into the standing frame several times a day for twenty minutes at a time and appeared to thoroughly enjoy it. Any longer though and Mia became distressed and made her discomfort known by mewing or screaming.

Mia was also being seen by the visual therapist on a regular basis. Mia now had the mirror ball which she seemed to respond to and a light and sound ball which also seems to relax her, so it appeared she could see some things.

We would say to Mia that her fairies had come to keep her company when we switched the light on as it looked like the room was full of beautiful coloured fairies dancing around.

Mia had her fairies around her every night when she went to bed. If she was awake when it was time for Howard and I to go to bed we would leave them on. If she was asleep we would turn them off...though this invariably meant that at some time before the alarm went off one of us would get up to check Mia was okay and turn them on again.

It was of course almost impossible to have a daily routine with Mia, as every day could be so very different from the last. Her medication being the only definite routine she had, now down to twice a day, 8am and 8pm every day.

Her feeds were managed around contact and how settled she was at the time. If she was unsettled a feed would be delayed in the hope that she would retain it and not sick it up. There was no more bedtime routine, as, again, if she was unsettled we would keep her in the same room as us to monitor her. There were no more spontaneous trips out, not even to the shops.

Caring for Mia was, though very rewarding, at times, very demanding and utterly exhausting.

We especially appreciated the help given by Sharon and her family at this time, which allowed us an occasional break to "recharge" our batteries.

At the same time though, I knew by now that at some time in the near future I would be letting Sharon know that we wanted to keep Mia forever. That I would be asking the departments involved in Mia's care to disregard the plan for Mia to be placed with either Sharon or another family so she could be adopted, in favour of staying with our family on a long term fostering basis. I knew from other people what Mia stood to lose through adoption.

I knew also that at that point it would change our relationship in regard of any future support Sharon would give us.

What I didn't know at that time was that Sharon and the mother had been meeting up for the odd cup of coffee in various cafes to discuss how things were going for Mia...that made an even bigger difference to the relationship Sharon and I had, for as much as she may have felt she had lost a colleague, I had lost someone I had trusted and respected to hold Mia's interests most high and now, once I'd learned about these meetings sadly, I lost that trust.

Chapter 35

By now Mia was having so many epileptic fits that we were visiting the hospital at least twice a week, either because she was having big fits that lasted more than a few minutes or because she was vomiting her feeding tube up and needed to have it put back.

As well as these 'emergency' visits she was still having her normal visits to see doctor Frankie as her epilepsy was once again becoming quite erratic, with seizures lasting anything from seconds to minutes, some small with minor movements, sometimes only a flicker of the eyes or a slight twitch of the face, others so big with her back arching and both arms stretched high above her head while her eyes opened so wide it was scary.

During this period Howard and I spent as much time as possible right beside Mia, monitoring her every move, yet trying to continue as normal as possible for the sake of Carl and Peter who needed normality so much, but who, particularly Carl, responded so well to Mia and her needs, running around and getting toys for her to play with, not understanding as he handed things to her that she had no way of clutching them as his baby brother did.

Carl had changed so much since he first moved in with our family. He no longer screamed and spat or bit. He was such a gentle little boy.

Oh no angel, but not the little devil he had been by a long chalk.

As much as Carl had calmed down, Peter had also thrived and it was so nice to see he showed little signs of damage due to his early life experiences.

Peter was so lucky...he had a chance of a good future with exciting things to come; pre-school; school; relationships with peers and girls. Marriage; a family...oh how I envied him his future and cried more tears for what Mia had lost.

Oh how I despised Mia's parents for the thieves they were...stealing so much from Mia while she was such an innocent.

I knew though that I had to get over this immense emotional burden that I carried around.

I knew that as long as I hated the mother, I would be unable to move forward with Mia.

Every negative though I had about the mother was a wasted thought.

It was a wasted second of my life.

If only I could feel absolutely nothing for the mother I knew that she would have no control over me; my family or how we lived our lives.

The mother wasn't really worth a nanno second of thought...negative or positive.

It took some time and a lot of practice, but we got there. Finally after having Mia in our family for over eighteen months, I felt nothing for the mother.

No hatred.

No liking.

No contempt.

No anything.

Only then I was free to just love my baby as I loved all my children...totally; openly; happily.

But this was a way off in the future...for now, all I had was this burning disgust in my heart for the person who had so wantonly destroyed such a special gift; such a special little lady.

Chapter 36

Bev, the health visitor was still a regular visitor to our home.

We got on well, Bev and I, having an established relationship built over the years of going to see her at the clinic, first with our children, then with all the little ones that had shared our home and our lives.

I had started taking Mia to the clinic when she first moved in to our home but some of the new mums got quite upset when they saw her have a fit, so it was decided that it would be better for Mia to be seen at home.

This arrangement suited me in many ways as trying to get to the clinic with three children under the age of four could prove difficult.

I was very lucky though because, with the support of the social services I had purchase a fantastic double pushchair. Not one of those little buggy things.

This was the Rolls Royce of pushchairs.

Great big wheels meant that I could go out regardless of the weather as it would just glide over everything, even slush and snow.

The suspension was great as well...no bumpy rides which could cause Mia to become startled.

It had two independent seats which could lay totally flat so Peter or Mia could sleep while the other was propped up.

Of course, we'd had a few mishaps when we first had this great bit of freedom giving technology...like the time when Peter was propped up beside Mia...he was such a little scrap and so inquisitive...he looked at Mia and before I could do anything reached for what must have been to him a great new toy...but it was Mia's feeding tube!

In the blink of an eye it was in his little hand...or more accurately, part of it was in his hand...the part that had come out of her mouth...

Poor Mia, poor boys...we had to go to the hospital instead of the park to get the tube put back down where it should be. Another learning curve travelled.

Bev was a constant source of reassurance when everyone else was busy and, time permitting, she would pop around to see how things were even if it wasn't one of the days she was due to see Mia to monitor her weight and development.

This arrangement also benefited Peter and Carl as it meant they were also weighed and had their health checks done at home and could be playing with their toys until the last minute, and off playing again the second they were finished with.

Chapter 37

Bev was pleased when she arrived one day to see Mia was feeding better than she had been a week earlier.

The week before she had been quite sickly and had lost a couple of pounds...now she had gained and was just over 24 pound, which was good.

But of course, with the good comes some concerns.

I knew that soon social workers would start to discuss Mia's weight.

They would start to assess the suitability of our home for Mia's long term future.

Actually, I don't suppose they would discuss our home as at that time we hadn't told them how we felt.

I just knew that they would be thinking of finding her a permanent home once the final hearing had been heard as I felt sure no judge would allow Mia to return to the mother. Though this date was for now a fair way off the court case against the mother was still slowly approaching. It was quite possible that social services would probably be making their plans already.

A plus side, if there are any plusses is that not everyone wants to care for a child with such profound disabilities so apart from Sharon there was possibly no-one else on their books waiting in the wings.

After all, I hadn't wanted to care for her in the beginning had I?

I knew I would have to speak with Howard and our children soon about what we could do to our home to make it more Mia friendly.

We would probably have to have a stair lift to get her up to one of the bedrooms...much better than sleeping in the playroom which she had taken over as she was now too heavy to carry up to the nursery.

We would need a tracking system from her bedroom to the bathroom, or perhaps we would have a hoist in the bedroom and bathroom. Maybe we would need an extension on the side of our home...the options seemed endless but as a family we would be happy and willing to consider anything and everything if it meant keeping Mia with us.

These were just a few things to ponder as there was also the question of access into our home with an adult sized wheelchair at some time in the far distant future.

For now though, we just had to live each day as it came.

Enjoy the moment.

Chapter 38

Contact was by now quite a contentious issue.

Not only for me, knowing that Mia would be neglected while with the mother, though not as bad as she would have if it were not for the fact that a social worker was always present, but also for Mia who seemed to know when it was a contact day, even though she had no language.

The only time Mia seemed truly content was when we had days that were just about our family, or our family and Peter and Carls grandparents, who were still very much on the scene and helping by having the boys stay some weekends.

Another problem that arose for Mia, apart from the fits; difficulty in feeding and drinking, was her size.

Many people on high doses of medication (Yes I know this can be depending on what medication it is), tend to gain weight.

And gain weight fast. It is unfortunate that if you are on certain medications and immobile, you will gain weight even faster.

Mia gained weight.

Sometimes, due to the size of her Mia would get sore in the creases of her poor little neck (she's still only a baby, so it's a small neck, just a tad chunky).

Following consultation about the sore areas around Mia's neck with Doctor Frankie I collected a prescription for an anti-fungal powder to use in Mia's creases.

The mother complained if Mia had any sort of mark on her and this included any area of redness.

The mother would complain that Mia had a sore neck and would put cream on it.

This is how shallow the mother is.

I put an anti-fungal powder in Mia's bag when she went to see the mother so if there was an area of redness, the mother could put the powder on therefore drying the soreness up.

The importance of this was clearly explained to the mother...on several occasions by me and by contact supervisors. We need to keep the area dry...not moist.

The mother ignored this and would put cream on...even if there was no sore or red area the mother would cover Mia in cream which would then cause dampness and soreness...and an awful smell.

What is your problem...can't you do one tiny thing to make Mia comfortable?

Sometimes the mother would phone just to piss me off...or so it seemed, when I got telephone calls from her and the first words out of their mouth were "Can't talk for long, I'm on the mobile," followed by a quick "How's Mia?" and getting the dial tone immediately after they were told.

The mother was just so very rude.

The mother would then telephone social services and say I had refused to talk to her!

Oh how I wished I never had to speak to or see the mother again. Ever.

Chapter 39

The mother, as ever, was quite unresponsive to Mia's needs.

Countless times I explained through the contact book, having already given a practical demonstration at one of the mother's contact sessions, some of the physiotherapy Mia needed to have done daily.

The mother always appeared to remain immune to Mia's plight.

Every contact session I put swabs in a box so the mother could at least moisten Mia's lips, and found myself having to reminded her constantly that the swabs were there, in the bag for if Mia looked a bit dry around her mouth and how to wet them and wipe them around the inside of her mouth.

The mother remained oblivious to all but her own needs, while proclaiming for anyone who would listen how much she loved her child. How much she would care for their child when she eventually went back to live with them.

For now though...the mother wouldn't even change a nappy or give poor Mia a damp swab across the lips.

Of course, there was one thing the mother would always do...mostly with the grandmother in tow if I was to be present, and that was attend appointments.

The mother loved these...wallowing in self-pity at what was their 'lot' in life.

Telling everyone and anyone who would listen how it wasn't their fault what had happened...

No-body listened though.

Everyone had heard all this shit before.

For months now it had been self; self; self...

So it was no surprise for me to find the mother and the grandmother in the waiting room when I went to see Doctor Frankie.

Fortunately only the mother came into the consultation room with me.

Mia had been weaned off of one of her medications; it now had to be re-introduced, over a 4 week period, and we were to start weaning Mia off of a recent addition to her medications, over a 10 week period, starting as soon as possible.

This was very good news as I didn't like the effect the new medication had on Mia...she was being too sick again.

Because Mia was being so sick I had to go to hospital on an almost twice daily basis to get Mia's tube replaced, meaning the boys also had the trip to do if Elizabeth was out with her family and my daughter-in-law or parents were otherwise engaged.

Also, every time the tube came out it had to be re-inserted up the other nostril, which meant the dressing on her face being taken off and replaced on her other cheek. This caused Mia discomfort and damaged her skin.

Unfortunately it took two days before I managed to get the prescription and start Mia back onto the Ethosuximide which made such a good improvement to her epilepsy control.

On the first day there was not much improvement, there appeared to be a slight difference in her rapid eye movement and, in general, Mia had a good day, though we still had to go to the hospital again to have Mia's tube replaced when she vomited it out.

A few days later the nurse had to come out as Mia had a nasty red area to her left cheek. This seemed to be from where she had had the tape removed so often over the weekend due to the tube needing to be put back up her nose and down her throat after she was violently sick.

The nurse used some duoderm on her, which was like a skin that would remain on her face, with the dressing for the tube stuck to it. This meant that every time Mia needed the tube being changed, they would only be taking the tape off of this permanent dressing and not off of her skin.

Though this also meant that the tube had to be inserted up the same nostril each time; until the fake skin was removed and a new patch put on.

Whatever...I didn't mind so long as Mia was comfortable and she was not getting any more damage done to her face, because with the gentlest of hands and the best will in the world, no-one could stop the tape from marking her when it was removed.

Swabs were also taken at this time just to make sure she didn't have some sort of infection brewing.

While the nurse was here I told her about the vast amounts of bile that Mia had been bringing back over the weekend so she eased the tube out a bit.

No sickness after the next feed!

I hadn't realised that tubes could accidently be put too far into the stomach...right down to where the bile lays...so that as you take in any fluids, the bile shoots out.

Chapter 40

Sarah came out one day near the end of summer and asked me if I would take Mia to another contact session.

Everyone hoped that with the court date coming closer, the mother may at least try to do something nice for Mia. So, I went with Mia to contact to show the mother, yet again, what to do with Mia regarding giving her physiotherapy.

Mia became quite stiff when we went into the contact room and took some massaging before she relaxed. Once again I went through some basic routines and showed the mother what Mia likes, leaving Mia nice and relaxed after short massage.

While I was there the mother asked me if I thought reflexology was a good idea for Mia.

Wow...shit for brains is finally showing some interest in Mia...,

I told them I didn't know and the mother said they would send some paperwork to me about it.

Fat chance of that ever happening.

But the court date is approaching so...

And the answer is no...I never got any paperwork about reflexology from the mother.

Chapter 41

As the regime of physiotherapy and occupational therapy carried out at home for Mia progressed she became a bit more flexible.

We knew this was possibly only 'borrowed' time as with every new batch of epileptic fits she could go back so far and we'd have to start teaching her how to bend and hold toys all over again.

But for now, Mia was content with her daily massages and physiotherapy that the whole family took part in if they were home for a visit.

The mother continued to try to undo any good we did...refusing to have almost anything to do with physiotherapy when she had contact with her. In fact, the mother had very little to do with any personal care as well, saying that she would get involved in nappy changing etc when Mia was returned to her as she didn't think she should have to do anything like that while she was living with our family. Thing is...our family were not involved in her contact sessions so nappy changes had been left to the supervisors of each session while the mother popped out for a smoke.

Due to Mia's size she was still getting quite sweaty in her baby creases around her neck and at the top of her chunky little legs. Having been advised to use an antifungal powder which Doctor Frankie prescribed as this would work better at drying it up and sharing this with the mother I found I had to yet again ask the mother to use the powder provided in the contact bag but, though she had been asked so many times before not to use cream on Mia, she continued to do so.

This meant that Mia was still having an almost permanent sore and smelly area under her chin and around her neck in those baby folds.

Selfish git...why can't you just think of Mia for once in your life?

I think the mother was also annoyed at this time as Mia had changed her sleep pattern and now needed feeding at every contact, and by not using the powder it meant she could complain about the soreness every time she saw Mia.

The mother didn't like feeding Mia because Mia didn't respond to her very well at all and would whimper or cry and refuse her meals and of course would need to be cleaned up which was another little job the mother didn't want to involve herself with.

This was not a good thing from the mother's point of view as she felt she was being watched by social workers who didn't want her to have Mia and would be documenting everything she said and did.

This was not a good thing from my point of view either, because it meant that Mia would come home hungry as well as fractious...

Soon...please make it soon that contact would not be seen as in Mia's best interest.

Chapter 42

It was mid -summer now and Mia's epilepsy was once again becoming unstable.

We were also having more difficulty feeding her.

She now had a special tumble form seat to sit in which gave her total support when we were trying to teach her how to hold things, or if she was just relaxing.

This was much better than the bouncy chair she had been using as, though we had bought the best we could find, Mia still slipped down when in it and it offered little in the way of support for her weight.

Mia also had a special high chair which could be angled. Technology is such a wonderful thing.

If Mia was sat too upright while having her formula she would be sick. Yes...Mia was back on proper foods again.

Too laid back and she would be sick.

This new highchair could be pitched just right for Mia and, though still sickly at feed times we managed to cut that to a minimum...for now.

It was lovely to see Mia at meal times as now she could eat her food safely strapped in and not wedged on the settee or sitting in the push chair which, if she was sick, would mean we wouldn't be able to just go out as everything would need to be washed. It was also great for helping Mia with her physiotherapy as working on her hands was easier for me if I sat in front of her.

It still appeared though that the only time Mia had any real peace was when she slept, and even than she could go into a fit at any time.

We kept Mia with us later and later into the evening in order to monitor how she was and to try getting feeds down her.

We weren't to be lucky though this time as, towards the end of the summer Mia had to have a nasal gastric tube re-inserted.

We were back to tube feeds.

Chapter 43

Tom was still popping in to see how Mia was getting on, though by now, although I liked him, it seemed almost pointless to be stimulating her vision when everyone knew she couldn't see.

Oh how despondent can you get.

Think positive!

Think light and dark!

With hindsight and a more positive mind, I can see that much of what Tom did during his visits was good.

He reinforced as did everyone in 'team Mia', that she was getting on just fine. We just had bigger hiccups and larger hurdles to jump every now and again.

Three steps forward and two steps back…and sometimes one step forward and three steps back.

Tom taught me so much about how to stimulate Mia, even though we quite often went over the same ground, reasserting the same ideals and values, reassessing Mia's needs and how we could best meet them.

Yes, hindsight is a wonderful thing.

Unknown to me at the time, Tom was soon going to move on to another job.

I would meet him once more after he left. I would see him on the day I was told Mia would never be able to have any food other than what went directly down a tube.

But for now Tom was there and we were both busy trying to stimulate Mia with various toys as her lights were slowly gliding around the room and Mia lay on the floor with her 'fairies'.

We had different textured fabrics to place in her hands or rub gently across her face.

Mia was peaceful.

Chapter 44

Mia woke me up at around 3.30am.

She was having quite a large fit so I quickly telephoned for an ambulance.

Dear God...what is taking them so long?

Finally the ambulance arrived.

Howard had been in the street waiting for them while I stayed with Mia, watching her little body convulsing in the cot.

This was so scary...scarier than the last time.

Last time we went under 'blues' and they let me hold her.

Last time we just got into the ambulance and went.

This time...would we even get into the ambulance or would she be gone before they arrived...

This time once we were in the ambulance they gave Mia such a thorough checking over.

Mia was still having convulsions.

This time Mia was wearing an oxygen mask all the way to hospital.

This time... my heart was truly breaking with the pain of what she was going through...the enormity of Mia was once again hitting home.

It hurt.

It hurt so much because there was nothing I could do to help, apart from be there for her.

This time I was a spare body, trying desperately not to be in the way, while at the same time trying to give Mia the reassurance that I was there with her.

This time I did the unforgivable as well.

I didn't let the mother know.

Mia didn't need her to turn up at the hospital and cause her more distress.

Anyway, this time we were lucky.

Thanks to the fantastic staff at the hospital Mia was checked over, monitored, and allowed home the following morning having slept quite peacefully while I kept vigil beside her with the nurses.

Not that we were home for long as after having her first feed Mia promptly vomited her tube out!

The following day Mia vomited her tube out again as she finished her first feed.

Shit!

I telephoned triage to tell them I would be coming in with Mia, not expecting the response they gave.

Doctor Frankie had already phoned the ward and explained to them how Mia's epilepsy was becoming unstable.

She had asked them to admit Mia so they could try to stabilise her fits and sort out her feeding, as she was being sick so often.

Having no option now, I tried to telephone the mother...praying that she wouldn't answer, to let her know I was taking Mia to the hospital but the line was engaged.

Great...I was so happy that at least she wouldn't be at the hospital when we arrived and I could settle Mia in nicely.

I could say in all honesty that I had tried.

I'd phone the social workers once Mia was settled and let them know and they could phone the mother.

I'd do that once Mia was settled...

I know it's not nice to have a sickly child but, a sickly child with a sicko mother in tow? I couldn't cope with both, I didn't want to cope with both so decided to settle her and leave the hospital before the mother arrived.

At least I could settle Mia into the ward in peace and quiet.

Once Mia was settled I left the ward, heading for home, just as the mother was arriving for her contact. Social services had quickly let her know so she didn't arrive at the contact centre as she would no doubt have complained about that as well.

The mother seemed harassed and asked how bad Mia was.

I told the mother that Mia wasn't "bad", she just needed to have her tube fitted again and to get stabilised on her medication.

The mother started to moan about not being told and I said to her "next time, answer your phone...then you will know what's going on won't you."

With that I walked out of the hospital knowing another complaint would be reported to Mia's social worker. Ho-hum...sometimes it was just too hard being 'professional'.

I couldn't be near the mother.

I didn't trust the mother not to twist something I said or did...and I didn't trust me not to say or do something I'd later regret.

Chapter 45

As Mia was growing into quite a large baby, partly due to managing to keep some of her feeds down...the projectile vomiting was now a distant memory; partly due to her medication and, of course, partly due to the fact that her only movements were when she had an epileptic fit, it was felt that I should not be carrying her up and down the stairs.

There are quite strict rules about manual handling and there is a weight limit which we are not allowed to go beyond for risk of back injury to ourselves, which may mean we are unable to carry out the tasks we need to as foster carers, as well as the risk to the child you are handling.

Mia's social work team were just so on the ball.

They arranged first for a hospital cot to be delivered and we converted part of the play room into a bedroom for her.

The new cot was a God send as it meant she could be high enough to ensure minimal lifting for me and Howard and maximum safety for Mia.

Shortly after this I had a new electric bed supplied for her.

This was brilliant!

As Mia was sadly back on nasal tube feeding after attending an appointment at Great Ormond Street hospital and undergoing a 'swallow test', which showed that food was getting into her lungs, and still on copious amounts of medication, we had a monthly delivery of syringes to our home.

Boxes and boxes of the things from 50ml right down to 1 ml for exact measurements of feeds and medication.

When the new bed arrived we discovered that if we had it at the right height we could secure the fire guard, when stretched out, around the bottom of it, giving a safe storage area for all her medical needs; nappies and food supplies, which we also had delivered in bulk.

And of course, Peter and Carl had a new toy, as every day they would sit at the bottom of the bed for a 'ride' up and down with Mia.

Another good thing to happen was the measuring up for a new bath chair. It's quite amazing the amount of equipment that is needed for one small child with disabilities.

Several designs were considered but we settled on one that was like a sun bed with soft straps to hold Mia safe while immersed. This would leave my hands free to wash her and splash water over her without fear of her drowning.

It also meant she could lay in the shade while out in the garden and get a cool breeze all around her, something she didn't get while in her pram.

Chapter 46

The last couple of weeks had been peaceful in that we only had Mia to look after.

Peter and Carl had been on holiday with their grandparents, so Mia had Howard and me to herself.

The day arrived when the boys were due home and we would once again become a noisy home with what were proving to be two healthy; happy; boisterous boys.

Yes, today would be a busy; busy day with lots of visitors what with the boy's home from camp and their grandparents staying for lunch, then friends arriving for an evening meal.

Our home was ringing with the sound of children playing and adults chatting. Mia seemed content with all the hustle and bustle and lots of attention she received from everyone. She was still having little fits but they were so much easier to spot now that her eyes don't dart all over the place.

It didn't matter what problems we met through our work with the various children we had looked after over the years, we had managed to overcome them.

None of these problems had been insurmountable.

The mother appeared to be though.

The mother phoned just as our friends went home after a lovely evening.

The mother was now pretty annoyed having been informed that her other children, who no longer lived with her, were to be given contact with Mia.

I had yet to spend any time with the mothers other children when the mother wasn't there. I had met them briefly, before they stopped living with the mother, when I had been to contact trying to get the mother to do some physio therapy with Mia.

The son was a sullen looking child...the daughter very quiet. Both I guessed were aged between nine and eleven years.

I had never met the paternal grandparent that was to bring them into our home so they could see their baby sister.

The mother: Has Mia's sickness stopped?

Me: No

The mother: Ahhhh. Would you say she's more alert?

Me: She seems to be, yes.

The mother: Have you heard anything about the contact for Mia and her brother and sister?

Me: No, have you?

The mother: Probably. I might have.

The mother then went on to tell me that the ex-husband, who the children now lived with, had a new girlfriend. According to the mother, the ex-husbands new partner had a drug habit and as the ex-husband had a high powered job they would just find it too embarrassing to enter our home.

The mother went on to say that there was a lot of abuse coming to light that was going on but that it was all just being accepted by the social services, and that her daughter would just have to get over that.

The mother informed me that her daughter will hold Mia but her son won't.

The mother then started to discuss the possibility of having a home assessment in my home. Stating that she had heard from one or two people that I had refused to even think about it, but she wanted to hear that answer from me.

What could I say?

Me: No way. My husband wouldn't allow it. In fact not one member of my family would agree to that happening.

Did the mother think for one second that I would l allow them to soil my home by letting them set one foot past the door? I didn't even want her on my driveway!

The mother: I'm looking at a unit that Mia will stay at for six weeks and I will be there during the day.

Me: Who cares for Mia overnight?

The mother: It's a specialist unit with medical staff that take over during the night as it's a long way away.

Me: And do you think that's in Mia's best interest?

The mother: It's a long way away. This place is in London. Three days contact is worse for Mia than being somewhere that I can see her for five days. I'm determined to do this assessment. Will Eve just turn up unannounced or will you know when she's coming if she brings the kids to contact? The reason she's against me is because you refused a placement for her because of Mia.

Me: I work for Eve. She's Peter and Carl's social worker and a bloody good one.

The mother: Oh. There's something about her I don't like – I'm sickened by what is going on. I don't like Mia's hair cut. It's quite short. I don't know who cut it, but I don't like it. Next time it's cut it's not to be so short or I want to be there.

Me: It's cut short because I'm concerned about having to put it up in bobbles in case she gets a headache and can't tell me.

The mother: There are other children as bad as Mia and you can buy big bobbles so she won't know it's up.

Me: Next time it's cut, if it's here, you won't be, because you can't come here.

The mother: One sides shorter than the other

Me: I'll get the girl round to even them up

The mother: No I don't want it even shorter. Children with problems always have the same hairdo, so having it done in that sort of style makes her look more not normal. I've been shit on by different people for long enough. Now I just want to be more involved.

At this point the mother ended the conversation.

Which, to be honest, left me wondering how much the mother knew about what was happening regarding contact.

And left me wondering how little I knew about an assessment. Surly they weren't going to give the mother an assessment.

All I knew for sure was that this was one angry mother.

The anger was not because Mia had been so badly damaged when her little body was shaken so violently.

Oh no...Their anger was because the mother had no control over any of her children's lives.

Chapter 47

Towards the end of the summer I heard some encouraging news at Mia's review meeting...the Guardian-ad-litum was strongly opposed to a parenting assessment of the mother. I think most people were opposed to it as the results had now come in regarding the outcome of the mother's psychiatric report. However, until the final hearing there was no option but to proceed along the lines of having this in place so as not to cause any further delay in deciding Mia's long term care and where she would be living.

Of course this meeting started with the mother complaining that not everything she does when having contact gets written down and things she doesn't do were reported by the family care workers who supervised the contact.

She complained that these workers were also documenting conversations she was having with her mother and not what was happening with Mia at these times.

The mother also complained that she felt I had taken over the role as Mia's mother and had got the telephone contact with her stopped. This was something I had been forced to do in order to protect myself a few weeks earlier, after one too many complaints had been put into the office accusing me of saying things I hadn't said.

Mia's feeding problems had become worse and we were still awaiting an assessment to see if she would need a gastrostomy for long term feeding. But a positive at this time was that she was more pliable so when she was 'well' we got more out of each physiotherapy session.

The social worker discussed contact and explained that Mia didn't cope at all well with the current amount of visits to see her mother. Preparing Mia for these visits was difficult because of feeds, dressing, additional water flushes and the extra medication she was now taking.

It was pointed out that Mia would often became distressed and whether this was due to being tired, her medication or her feeding regime wasn't the issue...the problem was, when Mia became distressed she was more likely to fit...a discussion around cutting the number of contact days ensued with the recommendation that she have two longer sessions a week...but...if the court granted a Care Order and declined the parenting assessment then Mia's contact would need to gradually be reduced in line with the Departments Care Plan for adoption or long term care.

Mia had already been presented to the Best Interest panel and they had deemed adoption to be in her best interest with long term care being considered if no prospective adopters could be found.

With Mia's long term health concerns and an uncertain prognosis regarding how long she may live adoption seemed quite an unrealistic option. Not many people want to be introduced to a child with a view to adopt when they haven't had a previous relationship with that child so I felt a little easier in feeling Mia would be staying in our family for quite a long time.

Howard and I now formerly wrote to ask if we could be considered as her long term carers…and were looking forward to contact being reduced over the coming months.

Chapter 48

Shortly before the best interest meeting Doctor Frankie asked me to complete a two week diary which could be used not only for the Best Interest panel but also in court should the mother appeal any recommendation the panel might make.

It was necessary you see, to fully show the extent of Mia's disabilities and the high level of care she required on a daily basis.

Now; in all honesty, we just lived our lives.

Mia was a huge chunk of our lives but, we had other children to care for as well...Peter was thriving and showing no ill effects from the head trauma he had received, Carl was being assed as he still displayed autistic tendencies, but we were well supported with this placement, as their maternal grandparents were very actively involved and looked after them some weekends, with a view to having them placed permanently at some time in the future.

So, I figured the best way to do an accurate diary of our daily lives was to just switch the computer on the moment I got up and just log events as they happened.

This turned out to be something of a headache though because, though we lived our lives neither Howard nor I had given any consideration as to how we lived and the amount of time Mia took up in any given day.

I tried so hard to keep the diary going but after six days I had to admit defeat.

Writing the diary wasn't the problem...reading it was!

Even with having a weekend away from all the children I felt exhausted just reading any day's events.

These were our normal routines.

This was how we lived our lives with three young children...easy...until you read it all back.

Chapter 49

MIAS DAY

Thursday

00.30 Mia has her fifth feed for yesterday. She is sleeping peacefully.

01.00 Howard and I go to bed.

03.00 Mia vocalising. Go in to check she is okay, have a cuddle and settle her down again. Go back to bed myself.

06.00 Check Mia is okay and change nappy. Go down to prepare feeds for the day. Put the last wash from yesterday in the tumble dryer as it was all towels.

06.30 Prepare syringes for aspirating and feeding.

06.45 First feed given, (as with every feed and every medication, this means aspirate the tube, once certain the tube is in the right place, flush the tube, then feed Mia, then flush the tube through again). Mirror ball on to keep her calm. Mia goes back to sleep.

07.15 Have a quick shower and help Howard with sorting the other children out.

07.45 Prepare Mia's medication, check syringes for aspiration and flush.

08.00 Mia has her medication. Mirror ball back on to help her relax.

08.20 Wash and dress other children, (Howard helps), get dressed myself.

08.40 Howard goes to work. Check Mia. She's been sick. Bathe her and change the cot.

09.15 Mia bathed but not dressed, wrapped in towel and relaxed. First lot of washing for the day goes on. Elizabeth arrives to baby sit; I leave her to dress Mia as do not want to rush her in case she's sick again.

09.45 Mia dressed, lying happily on settee.

10.00 Mia mega soils, all over herself and the settee. Mia bathed, changed and put into standing frame. Towel and two pillows ready for next wash, along with Mia's clothes. Settee washed and disinfected.

10.35 Back physiotherapy for Mia

10.45 Prepare syringes for aspiration and feed. Put Mia into highchair.

11.00 Mia has second feed. Mia settled and went to sleep in her chair. Hang out washing. Put second load in machine.

11.45 Mia collected for contact.

12.45 I get home. Thanks Liz for doing the laundry and looking after the children.

13.00 Grab some lunch and feed other children. Check if baby needs nappy change and change him. Howard comes home for a cuppa, the adult company very welcome! Howard helps with the other children and gives the baby his bottle.

14.20 Mia returns from contact. Quick chat about how contact went, and prepare syringes for aspiration and feed. Mia is given five minutes back physiotherapy by Elizabeth and put into her highchair, but is quite unsettled. Aspirate Mia and give her the second dose of reflux medication.

14.30 Mia has third feed. Quite an unsettled feed, Mia making quite a lot of noise. Put Mia on the settee to rest.

14.50 Play with other children.

15.00 Mia sick. Mia bathed. Three year old also bathed because "Mia is". Two vomit covered bath towels, two pillows and Mias clothes put into washing machine. Settee washed and disinfected. Hang out second load of washing and bring in first load. (Lucky it's a nice day). Have a drink of water and play with children.

15.45 Mia in sensory corner. Still a little vocal but settled and appears content. Sit in the garden watching other children playing and relax for five minutes.

16.15 Physiotherapy with Mia. Three year old fostered child joins in and helps Mia bend and stretch her legs. Mia quite flexible and appears to be enjoying herself.

16.40 Mia peaceful on pillows and towel on the floor as settee still damp. Spend time with other children, playing and then prepare their dinner.

17.20 Howard gets home, (late). I'm feeding one of the other children with one hand, and giving Mia a foot and leg massage with the other, so he makes a cuppa.

17.40 Mia is settled and the children fed so we sit in the garden and relax for a while.

18.00 Mia in the standing frame. Peaceful. I prepare her feed and check syringes for aspiration and feeding her. Howard is with the other little ones in the garden and hangs out the last wash.

18.15 Mia has her fourth feed. Sits quietly in her seat when she has finished. Howard has been seeing to the other little ones, as he is bathing the baby, the three year old wants another water play as well.

18.50 Howard puts little ones to bed. Mia is sick, luckily only a little so it's only one more towel for the wash. Mia has a wash and settles on the settee to rest before getting ready for bed.

19.00 Mia very vocal and needing attention. Howard gives her a cuddle and some back physiotherapy before getting her into her babygro. I am trying to prepare our dinner, but Mia continues to be unsettled, she has been having vacancies and small fits for about twenty minutes. I take over from Howard and comfort Mia.

19.50 Howard takes over with Mia while I prepare her medication and syringes.

20.00 Mia has her medication. Initially she is quiet, but within five minutes she is vocal again and quite disturbed. Howard comforts her while I try to continue with preparations for our dinner.

21.00 Mia is quiet and so goes to bed. Howard and I have our dinner.

21.30 Check Mia. She's sleeping peacefully. Get some tidying up done and do some ironing.

22.15 Check Mia. She's moved around in the cot. Move her so she is straight. Still sleeping peacefully. Time for a quick "chill out", we just sit and chat.

23.15 Check Mia. She hasn't moved since last checked. Prepare her last feed and check syringes for aspiration and feed.

23.35 Mia has her fifth feed; she stays asleep and is very relaxed.

24.00 Wash bottles and bring the last of the washing in. Put the washing machine on.

Friday

00.20 Go to bed.

0.5.30 Mia has slipped off her pillows. Howard makes her comfortable again.

06.30 Check Mia, she's asleep. Prepare feeds for the day. Washing not done, because the machine door wasn't shut properly. Shut the door; check syringes for Mias first feed.

07.00 Mia has her first feed; she's still asleep and looks very peaceful. Change her nappy and she doesn't wake, just stirs a little.

07.30 Have a slow shower. Howard is getting on with feeding the children. Check Mia. She is awake and vocal! Put mirror ball on to try to calm her.

07.50 Sort Mias medication and check syringes.

08.00 Mia has her medication. She is quieter now. Change beds and get other children washed and dressed ready for contact.

09.00 Mia goes into her standing frame, very content. Take out washing and put next load in.

09.30 Mia has been in her chair for the last 10 minutes, very contented. Mia has her second feed. We have to give feeds early on certain days to fit in with contacts.

09.45 Other children collected for contact. Finish feeding Mia.

10.05 Mia sick. Mia bathed, wrapped in a towel and laid on settee to relax. Minimum amount of movement is used when Mia is sick so I let her "drip dry" rather than manoeuvre her too much.

10.20 Washing hung out while Mia is peaceful.

10.25 Start washing and disinfecting highchair. Thought the floor had been missed but the vomit has gone past where the towel reached. Two tea-towels needed to mop up the footholds of the chair. Put towels and bed wear by washing machine. Wash and disinfect carpet. Mia is quiet and I am chatting to her while doing this.

10.40 Mia has gone to sleep. Not dressed yet and still wrapped in a towel. Very peaceful so I'll not disturb her, just hope she doesn't empty her bowels!

10.50 Speak to Sharon about Mia's vaccinations.

11.00 Phone surgery to book appointment for MMR (post court case).

11.10 Mia still resting peacefully. Hang out the washing and get some housework done.

11.45 Mia is still asleep but I have to wake her to get her ready for contact.

12.05 Prepare feed and syringes for Mia's third feed. It really is too early, but leave it later and Mia will be late, skip this feed until after contact and it will be at least seven hours between feeds.

12.40 Mia is quite distressed. She is put into the car and as Jen drives off she is sick. Jen stops the car and I clean Mia up, luckily it's only a little bit and only on her bib. Mia then goes to contact but is crying.

From contact Mia is going to Sharon's for the weekend as we are going away.

Sunday

20.30　Mia arrived home. As she was asleep she went straight to bed.

20.50　Mia awake and vocal. Bring her downstairs.

21.45　Mia quiet so put her back to bed with the mirror ball on to relax her.

23.30　Mia very relaxed but still awake. Fifth feed given. Light turned off and Mia settled for the night.

Monday

00.15　Mia sick. All bile. Mia washed and changed. Bed changed. Mia settled to sleep.

01.20　Mia sick. Mia washed and changed. Bed changed. Tube checked and eased out a little as it is too far in, all Mia is bringing back is bile. Aspirate tube to check it is in stomach. Settle Mia back for the night.

02.00　Make bottles ready for first feed, giving Mia chance to be sick again if she is going to. Put all dirty bedding and towels into washing machine.

02.30　Check Mia, she's peaceful so I go to bed.

07.15   Heat bottle and check syringes for first feed.

07.30   Aspirate tube, give Mia her first feed. She is still asleep.

08.00   Aspirate tube and give Mia her medication. She is still asleep so I have my shower and then help Howard with giving the other children their breakfasts and getting them washed and dressed.

09.20   Hang washing out. Put second wash on. Check Mia, she is awake.

10.00   Bathe Mia and get her dressed.

10.40   Mia goes into the standing frame. Very settled and content. Happy babbling.

10.45   Prepare feed and check syringes ready for feed.

11.00   Mia has her second feed.

11.15   Stop feeding Mia as other children go out for contact.

11.20   Finish Mia's feed and get her ready to go out.

12.10   Take Mia out to town. We need to collect Mia's medication from the chemist as well as collect a repeat prescription from the surgery.

13.10   Back from doctors and chemist. Not all the medication was ready so we will have to go out in a couple of days to pick up the rest. Have a quick coffee with Howard and hang the washing out.

13.15   Other children arrive home.

13.25 Mia has her physiotherapy. Very happy and relaxed.

14.00 Mia goes into her standing frame. Three year old playing around her. Mia appears to be following the noises being made.

14.20 Prepare feed and check syringes. Aspirate Mia and give her the second dose of reflux medication.

14.30 Mia goes into her highchair and has her third feed.

15.30 Mia lays on the settee and has a sleep. Time to play with the other children, put the second wash out, and get some housework done.

17.00 Amazingly peaceful afternoon as far as Mia is concerned. She has just woken up and is vocal but settled. Prepare feed and check syringes..

17.15 Howard gets home, we have a quick coffee and he takes over with the other children. While having a coffee I give Mia her back physiotherapy then put her into her highchair.

17.30 Mia has her fourth feed.

18.00 Mia content and in her standing frame. I prepare dinner and spend time with all the children and Howard. Little ones are washed and ready for bed.

19.00 Little ones go to bed, Howard and I have our meal. Mia in her sensory corner, very peaceful.

19.50 Prepare Mias medication and check syringes.

20.00 Mia has her medication.

20.30 Mia is washed and prepared for bed.

20.50 Mia taken to her bedroom. Mirror ball put on. Mia is very content and quiet.

21.30 Mia is asleep so mirror ball switched off.

22.30 Mia is awake, quietly vocal but not distressed. Mirror ball put back on.

23.30 Prepare Mia's last feed. Check syringes.

23.45 Mia has her fifth feed. Very settled and quiet.

Tuesday

00.25 Mia is settled and asleep. I prepare feeds for today, then go to bed.

07.20 Howard has warmed Mia's bottle and checked the syringes for me today.

07.30 Mia has her first feed. Howard prepares her medication for me.

08.00 Mia has her medication. Settles to sleep straight after this.

08.15 Have a quick shower while Howard is sorting out the other little ones.

09.00 Mia is still asleep so I get on with occupying the little ones and housework.

10.00 All the children have a bath. Mia went in with the three year old, she seems to like the noise and sensation of having others in the water with her.

10.30 Bring yesterday's washing in and hang out first load for today.

10.45 Mia goes into the standing frame. I prepare her second feed and check syringes.

11.00 Mia has her second feed. She sits contented in her chair with her piano under her hands.

11.45 Mia is collected for contact. Her nappy area is checked to ensure there is no nappy rash. All is well so Lyne takes her to contact.

11.50 Time to spend with the other children and catch up with the housework and laundry.

14.25 Mia returns from contact. Issues are still being raised about a nappy rash, so Lyne and I check Mia's nappy region, there is no rash. Mia is a bit fractious.

14.35 Feed, anti reflux medication and syringes prepared for Mia's third feed.

14.50 Mia is put into her highchair and has her medication and third feed.

15.20 Mia is sick. Strip, wash and change Mia. Wash and disinfect highchair and carpet. Put towels into washing machine. Mia is distressed so we sit and have a cuddle while I talk to her.

16.20 Mia is still distressed. She has spent time having cuddles and physiotherapy as well as going into the standing frame and sitting on her bath chair, (as a lounger). The only time she is quiet and fully relaxed is when I am holding her.

17.20 Howard gets home. He takes over with holding Mia while I have a break and make us a cuppa. We sit in the garden with the children. Mia is still vocal. Physiotherapy doesn't seem to do anything. Howard lays Mia on the settee, at last she quietens down. I prepare the other children's tea.

17.50 Prepare Mia's feed and syringes. Other children are eating.

18.00 Mia has her fourth feed. She is still vocal.

18.30 Bath Mia and get her ready for bed. Get other children changed for bed as well.

19.15 Mia has settled on the settee to sleep. Other children are in bed. Prepare our tea.

19.45 Check syringes and prepare Mia's medication.

20.00 Mia has her medication, she is still asleep.

20.50 Mia is still settled and asleep so I carry her to bed. Howard and I have our tea.

22.15 Mia is making noises. She isn't awake but appears to be distressed. Back slightly arched and face is rigid. This only lasts for seconds. She yawns, then, starts again. A foot massage seems to settle her, though she does not seem to have been awake or woken up.

22.50   Check Mia. Sleeping peacefully. Howard and I relax for an hour before getting things ready for the morning.

23.45   Make bottles ready for tomorrows feed.

23.55   Check syringes foe Mia's fifth feed. Prepare feed. Feed Mia.

Wednesday

00.45   Mia is settled. Howard and I go to bed.

04.50   Mia is awake and sounds distressed. Check nappy, she's clean. No sickness. We have a little cuddle and Mia settles down. Mirror ball goes on.

05.15   Back to bed.

06.45   Check Mia. She is asleep. Turn mirror ball off.

07.00   Make coffee and check syringes while warming bottle.

07.30   Mia has her first feed. She is very content. Nappy clean.

07.50   Check syringes and do Mias medications.

08.00   Mia has her medication. Very settled, mirror ball is on.

08.25   Howard has been seeing to the other children. I have my shower and sort myself out.

09.00   Mia has gone to sleep again. Spend time tidying round and being with the other children.

09.45 Mia has woken up. I get her washed and dressed.

10.05 Back physiotherapy given to Mia

10.15 Mia goes into her standing frame. Take highchair into the garden.

10.40 Give Mia some back physiotherapy and sit her in her chair.

11.00 Prepare syringes and bottle.

11.15 Other children are collected for their contact. Mia has her second feed. She appears to be very content and relaxed.

11.40 Mia is in her chair with her piano under her hands, she keeps pressing down on the dog key.

12.15 Mia has had hand and foot massage and now fallen asleep.

13.50 Mia has just woken up. Checked nappy, okay. I've laid her on some towels in the garden for some physiotherapy and to play with some small toys. (Encouraging her to hold things).

14.00 Check nappy again and change it! (And put the towels and Mia's clothes in the washing machine). Carry on with physiotherapy and playing with small toys.

15.00 Prepare syringes and bottle for next feed.

15.15 Aspirate Mia as usual. Litmus doesn't turn pink. Make several attempts to aspirate, most unusual, paper won't turn pink.

15.25 Give 5ml water, wait two minutes, aspirate, at last, paper turns pink. Mia has her third feed.

16.05 Mia is sick. Bath her, lay her on the settee to "drip dry". Wash and disinfect her chair.

16.35 Get Mia into nightwear. Mia is sick. Bath her, put towels into washing machine, wash and disinfect settee.

17.20 Howard is home. The children are eating their tea in the garden. Mia is in her sensory corner and Howard and I are in the garden. Mia is quite vocal but not distressed.

18.15 The baby is in bed. Three year old is playing in the garden. Howard relaxing on the settee with Mia, she's vocal so he is giving her a foot massage which seems to calm her down.

18.30 Prepare Mia's feed and check syringes.

18.40 Aspirate Mia's tube. Get nothing. Try again. No luck. Try using a 20ml syringe. Still no luck. Mia is getting restless. Leave her to settle.

19.00 Try to aspirate tube again. Nothing comes up the tube. Finally get clear fluid. Litmus stays blue.

19.15 Try 5ml of water. Mia coughs and is sick. Wash and change her.

19.30 Try to aspirate again. No luck. Get Mia ready to go to triage, pack medication, feed, spare tube, change of nightwear, baby wipes and nappies.

19.50   Phone duty officer, social services, to let them know I am going to hospital with Mia, the line is engaged. Leave for the hospital, Howard will phone the mother and duty officer.

20.15   Arrive at the hospital.

20.30   Nurse tries to aspirate tube, she has no luck as well. After several tries she syringes air into the tube and listens to Mia's stomach with her stethoscope. Tube is definitely in her stomach. Mia is quite vocal. Medication is now half hour late.

21.00   The mother arrived at the hospital and entered the ward without a social worker. As Mia is okay and I'm told the tube is where it should be I decide to come home to medicate Mia rather than take any chances of the mother twisting any conversation she has with me.

21.05   Leave the ward with the mother. The mother asks why Mia is shaking. I said I'm not a doctor and don't know, but that she was doing this during the last appointment with Doctor Frankie. The mother then asks if Mia would be warm enough outside as she was only in her sleep suit, but as it is warm outside (I only had a t shirt on), I told the mother that Mia would be fine. I also said at this point that the events would be noted and handed to social services tomorrow. The mother walked off and I put Mia into the car.

21.30   Home. I try to aspirate Mia again, have no luck, and as the nurse said everything is where it should be I give Mia 5ml of water then her medication. Mia is calm now.

21.45   Howards hungry so pops out for a take-a-way.

22.00   Mia goes to bed as she is calm. I put her mirror ball on. Howard and I have our evening meal.

22.25   Check Mia. She is asleep. Make feeds up for tomorrow.

23.30   Check syringes, warm milk and give Mia her fourth feed. She is quite settled but I'm not happy so will speak to community nurse tomorrow.

00.05   Check Mia, she is asleep so we go to bed.

I wrote the following letter to Doctor Frankie, enclosing the diary and asked if that would be enough for the court as it made me feel tired just looking at it.

Dear Doctor Frankie

Please find enclosed diary detailing a couple of days with Mia. I know you asked if I could keep a detailed diary for a week or two, but wondered if this would give you some idea of how busy life can be, and the commitment that would be needed by the mother should she have Mia returned to her.

Having switched the computer on first thing in the morning, and off last thing at night in order to be as accurate as possible, (and even then things like occupational therapy hasn't been logged as it is done with the physiotherapy), I have typed away for these few days, but I never really felt tired until I started reading what goes on in my life. It's strange that you can just get on with living and doing things that need doing and not realise just how little time you get to sit and relax.

I hope, short as it is, that this is of some help to you.

Yours faithfully

Thank goodness it was enough and we could just get back to just doing the job in hand.

As exhausting as it looks…this record is one of the best pieces of work I did while caring for Mia as it made all the difference when used as evidence to protect this very special little lady and secure her a future within a very loving home.

Even now, when I read this diary, I don't know how we did all that we did and stayed awake and alert.

I just know we did.

Chapter 50

Summer was fast coming to an end when we had a visit from Mia's solicitor and Guardian Ad-litum. During this visit all aspects of Mia's care and life were discussed.

Both the guardian and solicitor thankfully seemed to agree that a home assessment at the mother's house would not be in Mia's best interest as she was still very poorly and kept being sick after feeds, (Mia even graciously demonstrated this for them!)

This was a very reassuring visit as far as I was concerned.

Mia remained fine for most of that day, though was still being sick, especially after one of her medications, which was the only oral medication she had.

Sadly, due to Mia being sick no oral feeds were given some days and she had to have everything through the tube.

I knew of course that sooner or later I would be told once again that Mia would be only tube fed. I just didn't want it to be yet.

Slowly the days passed with all Mia's feeds going down the tube...and back out of her mouth. I knew the time had come to give Doctor Frankie a telephone call. I couldn't put it off any longer.

I spoke to Doctor Frankie and dietician about Mia's fits and they both agreed that it was best to discontinue with all oral feeds for Mia for the foreseeable future, also to reduce her tube feeds to 4 a day.

This gave me a glimmer of hope...perhaps it was just the amount of food Mia was having that was making her so sick.

Maybe; just maybe if the amount was cut down Mia would tolerate normal feds again.

Ever the optimist, that's me.

I asked the mother yet again via the contact book to give Mia some back physiotherapy to try to get some of the mucus shifted for her.

Ever the optimist...

I also explained that if the mother wanted me to do anything with Mia then they should write it in the book.

I knew I needed to cover my back!

The mother sent back a note requesting reflexology if I think it will do any good.

Oh yes...the court date is creeping up...

The mother also wrote that she thought the feed Mia was on was responsible for her sickness as it may be too rich.

Mmmm...must have been listening to someone at some time.

Mia's need for lots of back and chest physiotherapy grew as she had so much mucus on her chest.

I repeatedly asked the mother via the contact book if she would do this for Mia, also reminding them, yet again that there were swabs in the bag as Mia can look a bit dry around the mouth.

Every request fell on deaf ears though.

Again and again I asked the mother via the contact book to do back physiotherapy with Mia as the feedback I was getting was that this simple act of kindness; of love, was not being carried out during contact.

Over and over I reminded the mother about the swabs as they did not appear to be getting used.

Lo and behold!

At last Mia came home from contact with the mother and... One swab had been used!

Bet they were told they had to use it.

Bet they were shown how to be just a tiny bit kind.

Chapter 51

As the summer ended I received a note from the mother demanding the return of all Mia's Christmas and birthday cards that had been received since she had lived with us; photographs we had taken and the book that was used to communicate during contact sessions. Though this book had not always been written in by the mother, I made sure to always write in it how Mia had been prior to leaving our home and make them aware of any appointments that she was to attend with us.

In the note that was sent home it stated that if I didn't comply with the demands that the mother was making, they would be handing this issue over to the legal department.

I ignored it out of sheer bloody mindedness really. How dare the mother threaten me and demand I hand over items that they didn't have an automatic right to.

Mia's Christmas cards belonged to her and had been put away safe to be put into her Life Story Book for when she grew up. Not that she would ever read it or understand it, but it was part of her history, something that, should she not be left with us, would help another family get to know her better.

I didn't know what the mother wanted from the book, but it was not sent again and I started a new one, though I continued to write as I always had. No demands were ever made for a copy of the next book and it was always returned with Mia.

A little known fact that I found out many months later is; if a foster carer provides a book that is used as a communication book between them and birth parents; and the foster carer is the first to write in this book; the book belongs to them. It doesn't even belong to the Department of Social Services and if they want a copy they have to ask the carer first.

Also; a birth family member may demand to have a copy of the book but, the carers words belong to them. Therefore; technically and legally, all I had to do was provide the mother, at some time, a photo copy of their words.

This I did with all my words blacked out.

To ensure the mother couldn't bring my words up I photo copied the book; blacked my words out and photo copied it again, a little trick I was taught when having to provide information but keep the children's identities anonymous when doing my NVQ in childcare.

Chapter 52

It was mid-September.

Peter and Carl had been taken out for the day by their grandparents.

Today was to be a day of mixed emotions.

Having briefly met the mothers other children, Mia's siblings, I was in a mixed mind as to how today would go. This was the day they would be visiting Mia in our home.

I had, over the past few days spoken several times with their father, who they were living with. Oh if only this was one of Mia's parents.

This father sounded so kind...so concerned for the wellbeing of his children and concerned for the wellbeing of Mia as well.

There was to be no social worker here while the children visited. This I already knew as I had been asked if I would supervise the contact myself.

I knew that the children would be accompanied by their father and their paternal grandmother. And I really should not have worried.

When I opened the door I was so surprised to see two beautiful children. No sullenness or shyness here. It was like seeing two different children to the ones I'd met before.

The children and their father and grandmother came in. Howard made drinks while I stayed with everyone and Mia.

Mia's siblings were relaxed and played gently with her, both holding her and giving her gentle cuddles.

I don't think I will ever find the words to describe the grandmother. She was kindness personified and so gentle and gracious.

I spent most of the time they were here chatting with the grandmother about everything and anything. She was interested to know how Mia was getting on and what was planned for her future.

Hoping no doubt it wouldn't be a return to the hell hole her two grandchildren had left behind.

I took lots of photographs and a short bit of cine film with the intention of sending them on at a later date.

But life happens. Things get forgotten and sometimes I am put to shame.

But that is tomorrow.

That is one of my tomorrows and one day I know I will pass the photographs on. One day I will thank that lovely grandmother for her kindness. A kindness that she showed not just today but also some months in the future.

But I don't know that yet.

Right now, this minute, I'm living today.

Not tomorrow.

I know nothing of the pain or emptiness that awaits me.

That awaits all of us.

Chapter 53

It was just as the autumn started to peep around the corner that a meeting was called to decide where Mia would be living for the foreseeable future. Apart from Sharon there had been no other family identified as wanting to adopt a child with such profound disabilities.

Carl had not long returned to pre-school after enjoying his summer break and was busy making new friends as well as playing with old ones.

New starts. That's what this was. A new start.

Howard and I were excited and anxious at the same time.

By now Mia had been part of our lives for well over a year and the thought that she may be moved to someone else was scary.

Even the thought of her returning to Sharon, her previous carer and her family, much as I respected the work they did with children who had disabilities, Mia was now our daughter as far as we were concerned, in all but name and, as she was settled, we felt she should stay with us.

The day of the meeting arrived. As it was easier to hold the meeting in our home, thus preventing the need for me to be away from Mia for several hours, I got up early and prepared the lounge for what was to be a large gathering.

People started arriving; Doctor Frankie; social workers; physiotherapists; Tom from education; Sharon and Mia's health visitor all sat at the table.

I sat as far away from Sharon as possible, simply because she had no idea what I was about to say and, I knew she wanted to adopt Mia.

The meeting started and everyone said their bit.

It was considered to be in Mia's best interest for her to be adopted...but I hadn't spoken yet.

"Howard and I want to keep Mia with us" I finally said.

All eyes turned towards me.

Sharon looked, surprise registering on her face.

I was asked if Howard and I were intending to apply to adopt Mia.

"No" I answered.

I knew I had to be strong now as everyone had said this was what would be best for her.

"Howard and I...and our whole family...we want to be considered as long term carers for Mia."

I felt the eyes in the room looking from one to the other.

Sharon looked a bit happier, but I wasn't about to give up.

"We feel that as Mia is settled...as she knows everyone here and is thriving, that we can give her everything she needs...and we love her. We love her as though she is ours already."

The room was still quiet; people were looking at each other for support...I don't know...all I knew was that I had started to speak and I wasn't going to stop now, too much was at stake.

"If we adopted Mia we feel she would be the ultimate loser. While she is within the care system, you all have a duty to provide her with whatever she needs to be safe and comfortable. Without that system in place Mia would not have had the cot; the bed; all the other equipment that she has to make her waking hours more comfortable, so quickly made available to her. Mia needs that support and I feel; we feel, she should be given it."

Finally I stopped speaking.

Doctor Frankie, dear, dear doctor Frankie, who I had so much respect for. Respect she had earned over the years I had been seeing her with various children we had cared for was the first to speak.

Her words, I feel, directed the rest of the meeting.

"I think Lorraine has considered all possibilities here. I am in agreement with what she is saying. Mia has certainly thrived while living with this family and, she will certainly continue to be cared for and loved,"

My joy meant Sharon's disappointment.

I couldn't look at Sharon, as one by one those around the table agreed with Doctor Frankie.

I wanted to cry with relief; I wanted to laugh and shout with the sheer delight of knowing that we were being supported, and supported at what could be a huge expense to the department.

I wanted to say something to Sharon but there was nothing I could say. It wasn't a battle...there were no winners here, well, apart from Mia, who was the most important person involved.

When everyone had gone I hugged Mia to me; telling her she was safe and would be living with us forever.

We celebrated that night.

What a victory this could be for common sense and compassion for this little girl.

I sat and wrote a letter to the head of fostering in our local office:

Dear Georgia,

Whilst we are aware that adoption is in Mia's best interest, Howard and I would like to be considered as possible long term carers for her, if an adoptive family cannot be identified. We have discussed this with extended family members, and they all feel that if Mia is to be in long term care, better that she is within a family who love and know her, than moving to a new family where relationships have to be formed.

Of course, we still had to wait for full acceptance from the top boss in social services...but at least now we had hope.

Chapter 54

At last, three weeks after her review we received an appointment for Mia to attend Great Ormond Street Hospital for her reflux appointment. This would decide her future as far as feeding was concerned but it was still a month away.

We also received an appointment for Mia to attend the epilepsy department at Great Ormond Street and this was in to be after Christmas so still quite a few weeks away.

Before her London appointments I took Mia to our family doctor for her regular check-up. He was pleased that her fits appeared to be improving as she was now having short lived fits and she didn't seem to be losing consciousness so much. Also, due to the medication we could almost time the fits as they mostly happened an hour after her first medications of the day and an hour before her last doses.

Because there had been concerns about Mia's reaction to one of her anticonvulsant medicines we were now weaning her off of it. This has to be done slowly or there can be serious repercussions so the doctor had slightly increased her Epilem at the same time. Though this made Mia drowsy there was a vast improvement in how she was when awake and physiotherapy was easier to carry out. It's all swings and round-a-bouts with epilepsy, trial and error, but at last things seemed to be going well again for her.

By far the best news we had though was that the findings of the mother's psychiatric assessment had been accepted by the judge...there would be no home assessment...there would be no return to the birth mother...and there would be a chance for Mia to stay in our family or, if not that, at least she would be with a family who would care appropriately for her for as long as was needed.

Chapter 55

Mia was twenty one months old when we went for her visit to the epilepsy clinic at great Ormond Street Hospital and it was while I was there that I learnt of the level of damage that had been done to Mia when she was just one month old.

Having been taken to our local hospital she'd been resuscitated and then ventilated to the Paediatric intensive care unit at great Ormond Street. A cranial CT scan indicated a recent haemorrhage. There was also severe intra-retinal haemorrhage but fortunately no sign of retinal detachment. Mia had been ventilated for eight days before being transferred back to our local hospital.

I learnt that Mia had her first tonic-clonic seizure associated with the head injury before being transferred to London.

Mia's consultant noted that she had not made much developmental progress. She was not smiling, not sitting independently, did not reach for objects nor hold on to anything for any length of time. Actually, listening to this consultant knocked home to me how poorly Mia was. Not because of what she was saying because I'd heard it all before from numerous other medical people involved in her care, but the way she spoke…I was now more concerned but at the same time comforted by this woman's honest and open approach towards me and the child I loved.

The consultant gave Mia a thorough check up and commented that the cardiovascular, respiratory and abdominal examinations were unremarkable.

She noted that Mia had roving irregular nystagmus (uncontrolled movement of the eyes) and also noted that Mia gave no reaction towards light stimulation, which though upsetting wasn't as bad as hearing that Mia's EEG recording was grossly abnormal, with a poverty of normal activity.

It was decided that further investigation needed to be carried out and a fluoroscopy study was to be booked. This is where they film a person swallowing food and liquid and watch the journey these items take…quite an amazing thing to watch as I was to find out. There was to be another EEG an MRI scan and another ophthalmology appointment to find out if anything was going on with Mia's sight as it now looked like she had lost her light and dark recognition.

Chapter 56

Our second Christmas with Mia was lovely.

Carl and Peter had gone to stay with their grandparents for a few days so Howard and I enjoyed the time with James, Claire and Mia; with our other children arriving for visits on Christmas day and Boxing day; and of course my parents came along as well.

Like on our first Christmas with Mia we took lots of photos of everyone; including pictures of Mia in her cot with all her presents around her. These had been requested again by the mother to evidence Mia had been given presents by our family again, though she received very little from her birth family members.

At this time we were also advised to evidence for the mother that we were actually more capable of looking after Mia than she was, even though the courts had already agreed to continue granting interim care orders every three months.

Sarah, as with all the professionals that were involved in this case, was aware of the stories that the mother kept telling about the quality of care that Mia was being provided with. Sadly, every time a birth parent makes an allegation it has to be investigated even when it is known that what has been said is just through malice.

Every allegation though needs to be checked just in case there is some truth in it; after all, even foster parents/carers, are only human and some of them are not nice people.

Sometimes; just sometimes a paedophile will manage to convince the local authority that they are a very nice person with all the right credentials to care for someone else's child.

Chapter 57

By early the following year Mia appeared to be very settled within our home, and of course we were by then used to having her living with us and managing all her medical problems quite well. We had got used to the monitoring not only of her epileptic episodes, but also checking how she reacted to the changes she needed in her medicinal regime from time to time.

We had some more set- backs in her epilepsy control and physical development.

Howard and I had taken a short break and, while we were away, Mia was started on a new anticonvulsant, which didn't agree with her.

Within six days of our return she was admitted to hospital as she had no head control and was very limp. She came home after three days, but was readmitted within two weeks as she had gone into a non-convulsive state, and needed constant monitoring while her medication was adjusted. Mia remained in hospital for sixteen days, at which point it was decided to wean her off this medication.

Fortunately this could be done within her home environment, which meant Mia would be more relaxed and settled...not on a ward with lights on all the time and sounds of other children playing noisily or being distressed for all the reasons children get distressed while in hospital. It took two weeks to wean Mia off the medication...Two weeks of close monitoring and so many prayers that she would be okay; that we would all be okay.

Once Mia was off the medication, she improved quite a bit, though was still a long way from where she had been the previous summer; a summer that seemed to be a lifetime away by now.

Mia had another loss.

She could no longer use her standing frame as she was no longer able to support her head.

However, Mia had one bonus... she could still manage to sit in her snug seat which was great as it ensured when we went out Mia was sitting with proper support.

Mia had also had an MRI scan at Great Ormond Street hospital just after Christmas...we were still waiting for the results which would give us a clearer picture of what was going on in this little one's head.

Chapter 58

It was also felt at this time that Mia needed more support, through medication, to help with her epilepsy.

When started on this, the dose was 1.25ml, which she tolerated.

However, when the dose was increased she became very sick, so much so that the dose had to be decreased.Though not for long as we ever so slowly began the process of increasing the dose by .1 of a ml until eventually she tolerated 2ml doses twice a day, the dose needed to give her maximum relief.

Mia was then admitted to Great Ormond Street for a 24 hour ph study.

This was to be followed by a videofloroscopy (swallow test) and EEG. Unfortunately, due to the wrong letter being sent out by the hospital, Mia's anti reflux medication wasn't stopped and the ph study had to be delayed.

The video fluoroscopy was carried out though.

A fluoroscopy, or swallow test as it was explained to me, is where a camera is put down your throat so the doctors can see what happens as you eat or drink.

Mia was placed in a chair once the camera had been inserted and we all stood by the monitor to see what happened as she was given the tiniest tip of a teaspoon amount of yoghurt.

It was amazing to watch as this small minute amount of food moved across Mia's tongue.

It eased down her throat...

Everyone's faces dropped...

It diverted from going into her tummy and straight into her lungs.

That was the end of the swallow test.

No-one was willing to take the chance that the next spoon would go into her tummy.

Mia would never enjoy taste again when eating a meal or having a drink.

Sadly, because of the results, a gastrostomy was recommended.

The only good thing about that was the nasal tube feeding would be a thing of the past...no more having to have the tube replaced if Mia was sickly and no more tape on Mia's face to hold the tube in place, which was great as partly due to the medication Mia was on, her skin was extremely delicate and marked so easily, even with micro pore the skin could tear.

Chapter 59

Then there were the results of the EEG Mia had, which necessitated an ECG as there were concerns that Mia had an abnormally slow heartbeat.

So much was going on for Mia and we were barely into the second month of the year.

Though Mia was settling into her new medicinal regime, her epilepsy was still poorly managed and she continued to have many seizures every day.

These changed over the weeks in size and appearance.

Sometimes they would be small, lasting only seconds, when she would become quiet and vacant.

Some lasted a few minutes.

The larger ones tended to include the raising of one or both arms.

Mia also started to show signs of distress in her facial expressions during the larger ones and would cry out in a shrill voice as she came out of them though settled fairly quickly afterwards.

Then Mia had some full body jerking fits, which started once she had been given some new medication to control the fits she was having.

Smaller fits continued to hit poor Mia, where her legs would become jerky, and her little body became rigid.

We had so hoped with the mew medicinal regime that Mia's quality of life would improve and, in some small ways it did.

The positives we had, no matter how small they looked for us, for Mia were milestones which she had to pass again.

Slowly we started to use her wedge as she got a little more head control, and slowly we worked towards getting her back into her standing frame.

Her vocalising improved, though she only used the one word, "mum".

The first time Mia had said "mum" was when Howard and I were waiting in a queue to be served in our local supermarket.

There were so many people standing around with their trolleys full of shopping.

Mia was quietly sitting in her wheelchair, facing me.

It seemed like she waited until it was almost silent; or maybe it was because I had never heard her voice before; but suddenly there came this low; oh so low and deep sound..."Mum"

People standing around actually looked over and the lady in front turned.

I was lost for words; just looking from Mia to Howard who was equally surprised to hear any proper word be uttered from her.

I think we both could have cried right there and then if we hadn't had such an audience.

Mia had been saying mum for a while now and though initially it had been only when needing a change of nappy or clothes, it now appeared to be when Mia wanted a cuddle, to be spoken to or played with. I could have cried with the thought that our baby girl was trying to communicate at last.

Not just making random noises...but saying my name.

I was floating on cloud nine.

Chapter 60

Mia had been with us for nineteen months when her second birthday came round.

As disabled as Mia was, by now she had a small circle of friends and had a birthday party.

Peter and Carl were here, our granddaughters, Elizabeth came with her borrowed children and the little girl from next door.

Elizabeth by now was caring for another baby who had suffered the same trauma of being shaken, a little boy of a similar age to Mia.

Here was a little boy with similar damage done to him at the hands of a parent.

Mia and Stefan would lay together in the sensory corner and be quiet.

Mia tended to have her fits and lean to the right; when Stefan had his, he tended to lean to the left so we knew that Mia always had to be on the right side of Stefan when they lay together.

Stefan was the only child that Mia ever reached for.

Whether this was deliberate or not I don't know, but we would often watch them together, laying peacefully, and notice they were gently touching hands.

Louise had made a birthday cake for Mia just like the one she had made the month earlier for our granddaughter who was the same age.

To see our granddaughter now, who as a two year old was getting up to all sorts, knocked home how much our Mia had lost.

Our Mia had lost her life. All hopes and dreams had flown out of the window with one selfish adult action.

I felt at times that Mia had been murdered at a month old, but didn't know how to move on.

There were balloons and party food and, when the cake came in with the candles lit, plenty of little volunteers to blow them out.

When the children who could remember the words to Happy Birthday sang, Mia made such a racket as well...it was as though she knew this was all for her without seeing any of it.

Friends and family were also considerate when buying Mia's presents.

She had toys that were small enough for us to fit into her hands and all different textures, from rubber to silk.

One of my aunts had been busy knitting cardigans for Mia. These cardigans were knitted for no other child though. These were an exclusive design.

From the front they were normal, button through with round or v neck. Always my aunt used pretty children's buttons and lovely pastel colours.

But the back...well, that also buttoned up as well but with flat buttons that wouldn't cause Mia any discomfort as she lay on them. Such a considerate thing to have thought of and then to have spent time adapting patterns...Mia was truly loved by all our family.

I had found that to dress Mia in anything that necessitated going over her head caused her and me problems...

Especially when she was sick; also, to get anything on that buttoned down the front meant easing Mia's arms at an angle she found hard to tolerate so now, where possible all her cardigans and dresses buttoned right down the back, as that way we could simply lay her into them.

Even Mia's t-shirts were adapted to open all the way down the back, courtesy of a friend who was very good with her sewing machine and never complained when new clothes were taken to her for alteration.

Louise had very thoughtfully made a sensory birthday card that Mia could feel as well, with raised candles on a raised cake and such small balloons attached to it. All made using different textured materials. This simple gesture brought tears to my eyes.

Once the children had all gone home Sharon popped over with a birthday present for Mia, bringing one of her fostered children with her.

Altogether, it was a lovely day.

Even Mia's epilepsy had appeared better controlled for the day.

Chapter 61

At this time Mia's physiotherapy, which had become difficult to carry out due to her sickness, was also progressing, and she appeared to enjoy her exercises.

So much had been lost...we had danced the three steps forward...two steps back tango.

Maybe now we could just do a quick step forward...and another one...and another one...

Then one day a miracle happened.

I was sat in the lounge; going through the normal routine of physiotherapy with Mia.

We had done the leg massage and the back massage.

I had massaged Mia's arms and neck.

I sat her in front of me; facing me while Louise sat behind her.

I started to massage her hands.

Mia was so quiet; just sitting there; Louise making sure she didn't topple backwards.

Our granddaughters were playing in the playroom with Peter and Carl, toys everywhere.

I was just chatting quietly and gently let go of her hands.

Louise wasn't touching Mia.

She sat.

Mia sat for about five seconds!

We were ecstatic.

Five seconds was like a lifetime...we had waited a lifetime for this and Mia...sat.

Louise and I had tears in our eyes and I phoned everyone I could think of to tell them.

Oh my goodness.

Miracles happen.

Shite happens too.

Mia never managed to sit again. But I guess, it was enough that she had experienced what she had.

Of course it remained impossible to have any sort of daily routine, apart from when Mia had her medication, as she was so unpredictable and could still be very sickly at times.

It was hoped that once Mia had had the ph study and a decision made as to how the gastrostomy was to be done, and then carried out, that things would settle down for her and a more structured routine could be formed.

Caring for Mia continued to be very rewarding, though demanding and tiring at times.

It could also be very frustrating to watch her struggle so hard to make, what for her is huge steps forward, only to have a return to "basics" after a bad spell.

But she was a very special little lady and our whole family love her so very much.

Surely that would be enough to help her win her battles.

Oh the naivety we live with.

The dreams we hold on to.

Chapter 62

It was a couple of months after our second Christmas with Mia that we were advised to consider allowing Mia to attend a children's hospice.

We already had a respite carer for Mia now so why would we need to access the hospice?

The mere thought of Mia going into a hospice filled me with dread as I wasn't aware at that time that she was going to die. Oh I know we all die at some time, and I know I'd had concerns when Mia first arrived that she may just die on me...but we loved her...she was part of our family and as such...nothing could happen to her!

For all Mia's health issues, she was a healthy baby and rarely suffered with colds and hadn't succumbed to any childhood illnesses, so why should we look at the possibility of her going into a hospice?

It was carefully explained that many children go into the hospice to give their parents much needed respite and we were asked to visit one local to where we live so we could see for ourselves what a happy place it was for children to stay in.

I reluctantly agreed to go and went with Sarah one afternoon.

What a surprise I had. As we went in the first thing I noticed was the smell of the food as it was being prepared and cooked for the evening meal.

The staff we met there were lovely and friendly. We were shown around this amazing building; the offices as we entered, through to the large lounge and dining area. There were patio doors opening out onto a lovely garden.

We were shown a room like Mia would use if she were to stay and then shown the hydro pool and smaller hot tub.

During my time visiting I was also shown the rooms that family members stay in if they wished to stay overnight and the television room.

Finally, feeling happy that I had come to see this lovely place, I agreed that Mia could stay for a weekend.

Peter and Carl went to stay with their grandparents while Howard and I stayed home with some friends we had invited to stay. We needed the distraction our friends provided and didn't want to be too far away from Mia in case we were needed.

Of course we needn't have worried because Mia settled very nicely into her room; I just missed having her near me; missed checking her throughout the night; missed holding her in my arms and smelling her baby scent.

I missed my Mia.

Chapter 63

Sadly for me this weekend proved too much. Even with the distraction of having friends stay and the freedom of no children I couldn't settle.

But...

The department decided that Mia should have another stay at the hospice to give Howard and me a break.

This time I insisted on being allowed to stay at the hospice. Both Howard and I felt we would have more rest and relaxation if we were at least in the same building as Mia and could be there to say goodnight to her.

Some months later Mia once again stayed at the hospice.

Peter and Carl were to spend the week with their grandparents while Howard and I stayed at the hospice with Mia.

It was agreed that Howard and I would stay at the hospice and we could have as much or as little involvement with Mia's care as we needed; as I needed.

Every morning we would check in on Mia before I drove Howard to work. I would then spend some time at home; some time visiting friends and then head back to check on Mia before heading back to pick Howard up from work and returning to the hospice for the wonderful food they prepared for our evening meal.

In the evening Howard and I would spend time with Mia, taking her swimming in the hydro pool or just sitting with her in the garden or her room. We had bought Mia a mirror ball and light some months earlier, which we always had in her room overnight...we called the rotating circles Mia's fairies, so each evening we would set her fairies flying around her room before leaving the staff to carry out the evening and night routine of medication and watching while we chilled in our suite or the grounds.

Truth be told, our week at the hospice was quite idyllic in that it gave Howard and I time to rediscover each other and just relax away from the everyday hassles of our life, while knowing that Mia had expert care from the wonderful staff.

It gave us time to re-evaluate where we were going and what we wanted to happen next.

It gave us the confidence to leave our beloved child with these oh so very special people when we headed off for our next holiday, which was to be late in the year as we tended to prefer a holiday in either October or November as the late heat we got from being abroad meant I had less cold weather to cope with.

Chapter 64

As we had formally asked to be Mia's long term carers Howard and I had to sit and discuss the reality of Mia staying with us for the rest of her life.

We both knew she would probably not grow to adulthood.

For some reason, probably because it was an age I'd heard mentioned while at one of her numerous hospital appointments, we thought she would live to around the age of seven or eight.

We figured if that was the case we could stay in the home we had then.

Of course it would need some changes being made to it.

First, our home was over one hundred years old.

There are lots of stairs, not only to get to bed, but also to get to the back of the house.

No matter where you went you had to use stairs.

Sitting in the lounge and you fancy a cup of tea; down three stairs to the play room...down another stair to the kitchen.

Time to go to bed...up the stairs, there's the bathroom and kids bedroom; up three stairs to the next lot of bedrooms; up another flight of stairs to the top bedrooms.

Our home was full of stairs, stairs, and then some more stairs.

We loved this house, our home.

Now we faced the prospect of having to move to ensure we didn't lose Mia if we couldn't adapt our home to meet her growing needs.

We considered all the options.

Obviously a nice big bungalow would be the ideal solution.

But though we had a look, we didn't see any that would be suitable for our needs...and certainly none large enough to cater for Mia's needs.

We had discussed having a stair lift put in which would take Mia to the first floor.

On this first landing were a double bedroom and the main bathroom.

This would be ideal for Mia as she grew because the landing was quite spacious as was the bathroom.

Unfortunately for Mia, because of her epilepsy this was not considered a good option because, if she had an epileptic episode as we were transferring her from the stair lift to her wheelchair, she may fall down the stairs.

It wasn't only the risk of Mia falling; she could take whoever was helping her as well.

We went back to the drawing board and came up with the option of a proper lift.

This was all new stuff to us, I didn't even realise at that time that you could actually have lifts put into normal family homes.

So we then had a man from some company to do with putting lifts into normal homes come to measure up.

Only problem was, we didn't have a normal home.

Being the age it is it is made of 'soft red' bricks.

Sure the house had stood for over a hundred years with nothing more than piles of shingle as foundations.

The rooms were pretty soundproof here as well because the walls were all brick, no studwork in this age house.

But...

Every wall I suggested a lift go on was no good.

They needed to be put on an outside wall.

The majority of our outside walls are glass.

Finally it was decided that the best place would be in the lounge, to one side of the fire place.

This would mean that the lift would come up to either our guest bedroom, or our bedroom.

Both options were unsuitable to us as a family.

And it would definitely prove problematic for Mia, as the bathroom is at the back of the house...down three stairs.

Howard and I discussed the problem of getting Mia upstairs some more and came to quite a drastic decision.

We would not move.

What we would do is build a two story extension beside our home.

It would be accessed from the lounge by taking out one of the large six foot windows that overlooked the garden.

We would have a large archway leading to a room that would be used as a sensory stimulation room for Mia towards the front.

The lift would be on the external wall, giving maximum space in the back of the room for manoeuvring any equipment Mia needed and go from this room to a bedroom that we would access upstairs by taking the side window out of our bedroom, putting a door in its place. We still had a large six foot window that faced the back garden so we wouldn't be without natural daylight.

Mia's bedroom would be at the back of the extension meaning she would sleep close to us, with access to an en-suite bathroom at the front.

There would have to be a hoist system installed that would take her from the bed to the bath.

We would also have patio doors put in the downstairs room which would make getting Mia in and out of the house that little bit easier.

Everything was coming together.

Sorted.

Chapter 65

Some mornings Mia overslept.

This was both a relief and a cause for concern as, if by some chance I'd slept throughout the night, I would be almost scared to look in on her when I got up.

She was so poorly.

What if she had slipped away during the night...alone...?

The thought didn't bear thinking about, but it was always lurking, somewhere deep in the back of my mind since we had been visiting the hospice with her.

Some days Mia would be very difficult to feed, even with the tube she would struggle and be sick. The problem with tube feeding and gastrostomy feeds is that you have none of the sensations of taste or texture...you just fill up. Mia couldn't tell me if she was full up until she vomited the whole lot back...we were back to lots of feeds being shared like this...something I thought we had seen the back of a while ago.

Poor Mia. How she was suffering at this time.

Small things that we all take for granted were a major bonus for Mia and she had overcome so much.

What hurdles she had overcome in her short life…and what hurdles she still had to get over.

One day soon though, everything would come crumbling down again.

We didn't know that then though.

No-one did.

Chapter 66

Howard and I had been sitting in the lounge having a cup of coffee while Mia slept peacefully in the playroom.

It had been a bank holiday weekend which Peter and Carl were spending at their grandparents…they were due home at some time in the early evening.

Howard and I had spent the previous day with our family, including aunts and uncles and cousins who all joined us for a relaxing day and family meal. Our granddaughters had played in the garden and Mia had appeared content in her pram listening to the noise around her.

Everything about the weekend had been just lovely.

We liked to relax with a word game at some point in the day which is what we had been doing as we drank our coffee…I usually found the most words, probably because words fascinate me.

Anyway, we finished our drinks and went to check on Mia.

She was lying peacefully in her bed.

The sun was shining through the bay window.

All was quiet and lovely in my world.

As I lifted Mia from her bed I asked Howard if he would get me some water and the bits I needed to aspirate her before giving her anything.

Howard returned with everything and, once aspirated I put some water down the tube.

Howard was sitting beside me on the settee in the bay window.

The sun was shining.

It was truly a wonderful day.

Mia was quiet.

Mia was very quiet.

I looked down at her as she lay in my arms...so peaceful.

I don't know why but as I looked I said to Howard "I think she's going."

Howard looked from me to Mia..."She can't be. Not yet"

But even as he spoke she was gone.

She had slipped away so quietly in my arms.

Howard and I looked at each other, neither knowing what to do next.

We both just wanted to sit there and do nothing. Just be on our own with Mia. Our daughter, as she was considered by the whole family.

We didn't cry.

We were too numb for tears. Too shocked because, though we knew Mia had a limited life span, we didn't know it was this limited.

I thought back to Thursday at the hospital.

"Take her home" the doctor had said, even when I insisted that she was 'proper poorly'..."Take her home and keep her comfortable."

Was the doctor trying to tell me something and I'd been too stupid to realise?

Numb; numb; numb.

I knew I had to do something.

Howard stood and, like a robot phoned my parents to let them know...

Howard then phoned the nurse at the hospital, only to be told to dial for an ambulance.

What good is a bloody ambulance?

He did as he was told, then hung up the receiver just as my parents arrived.

"Put her on the bed Lorraine" my mum said.

"I don't want to...I want to hold her."

I felt the start of tears that wouldn't fall.

My mum lead me over to Mia's bed and I lay my beautiful little Mia down.

She was almost yellow.

She looked just like a little wax dolly.

There was a knock on the door and suddenly a paramedic came running into the room.

She went straight to Mia and started to get something out of her bag.

"Please don't" I said.

"Please don't do anything to her.

I held out a list of all Mia's illnesses.

All those nasty illnesses one of her parents had given her in a moment of temper.

That poor paramedic's face as she read the letter I'd given her. She looked at Mia, then at the four people in the room and spoke into her mike..."It's too late...she's gone."

Chapter 67

Everything happened so quickly after that.

Social workers turned up; the police arrived in several cars; an ambulance and then my neighbour arrived through the back door.

At this time Howard and I had been taken through to the lounge to give our statements to the police and social workers.

The front of our home was taped off with police tape.

Because my neighbour came round the back that was also taped off.

Suddenly a policeman arrived in a different uniform.

He entered the lounge, a tall man with his hat under his arm. His voice was so reassuring and he looked so smart with all that silver on it. Funny what you notice without even being aware that you are actually going through this scene.

He stood in the doorway and asked what we wanted to happen next.

I asked that Mia be taken to the children's hospice so that our family could say their goodbyes.

Oh how naive I was. She wasn't mine to say what happened next.

He looked at me with concern and sorrow for what we were going through.

"I am so sorry" he said. "Mia will have to go to the morgue for an autopsy. We are treating her death as murder..."

Oh my God!

The look on my face must have screamed a million words...I didn't kill my child!

Immediately he started to explain, saying "It was only a few weeks ago we discussed what actions we would be taking when Mia died, as we knew she would. We are now going after the parents and hope to charge them with her murder."

He then apologised for having to tape the whole house off, explaining that Mia's bedroom was considered the crime scene...even though we'd done nothing, it was the crime scene because that is where she had died.

He explained that if we needed anything from the kitchen we would be taken around the outside of our home into the kitchen as they had a police photographer and forensic people in Mia's bedroom.

I remember thinking...rather distractedly...what will the new neighbours think.

What will everyone think as they pass our home and see the drive covered not only with our cars but also ambulance and police vehicles.

I vaguely caught the scene outside.

Several police were walking up and down in deep discussion.

The phone rang, it was our son. Edward.

"Is everything okay mum? Has something happened to Mia?"

Apparently one of his friends had been driving past our home and, seeing all the police and ambulance activity then phoned him to make sure everything was okay.

News travels fast in small villages.

I told Edward that Mia had died a short time ago and we would speak to him later as there was just so much going on at that time.

We would need to tell our other children.

Not now.

I couldn't think; could hardly talk let alone think.

That beautiful day passed in a blur of activity.

Finally we were on our own.

Howard and I. Sitting together but lost in our own worlds with our own emotions.

Chapter 68

It was to be almost two years before Mia's funeral could take place.

The course of action taken after Mia died was quite extensive.

First there was the autopsy.

Then; and this is what took so long, there were exhaustive tests to discover exactly why Mia died at the age she did.

Her mother had accused me of her murder. Not that I knew about that until much later while talking to the Coroners Clerk just weeks before the Coroner Court sat to consider all of the opinions and information that had been gathered over the past 18 months or so.

There were lots of people at the court, Social workers; team leaders; solicitors; expert witnesses, the Home Office Pathologist and the coroner.

Then there was me and Howard with our close family and friends for support.

The mother arrived with her mother.

Just before the mother arrived we were all asked to enter the court.

They had contacted the Coroner's Clerk and told him they didn't want to enter the building and walk past us if we were still in the lobby.

We all sat. My family and friends sat with me at the back.

The social workers, doctors and solicitors were sat in front of us.

The mother and her mother sat below the judge's bench with their backs to us.

The Coroner entered and took her seat.

The first witness stood and approached the bench, standing opposite the mother.

He was an expert witness. This was The Home Office Pathologist.

He stood there, not a big man, but when he spoke it was clear and definite.

I could have cried...think I probably did but it was all so surreal.

Without looking at the mother or grandmother he addressed me and Howard directly, looking across the court to the back row.

"I am so sorry for your loss. I have to inform you that Mia died as a result of a drug overdose..."

Oh Dear God no I screamed in my head. NO! NO! NO!

This man then said, in such a comforting, kind and gentle way...

"There was nothing you or anyone else could have done to prevent this happening. Her medicinal regime was so toxic...no-one knew how toxic it was..."

As clear as he was and as hard as I tried to focus, I couldn't hear. Everyone had been trying so hard to control her epilepsy and manage all of her other disabilities...there were just so many problems for her little body to take.

"...liver was failing...."

Everything had been shutting down which explained the jelly pee.

"...and because of that, every time you gave her 5 ml of ethosuximide, it doubled the dose of all her other medicines..."

The Home Office Pathologist was very clear in his verbal evidence that, whilst there was 'ethosuximide intoxication' there were sufficient natural explanations for this, that there was no suggestion of overmedicating and that in any event whilst this was present, this was not the cause of death.

Next I was called to give evidence.

I sat opposite the mother and grandmother.

I looked straight at the mother...I couldn't look at anyone else for fear of bursting into tears...But this person I could look at and remain like stone.

The coroner spoke.

She very gently asked me if I could talk about events of the day Mia died.

I looked straight at the mother and gave a narrative of everything that we had done since Mia woke.

I must have a nasty streak in me though, because as I got to the time when Mia died, I stared deep into the mother's face and said in a clear voice..."Mia was so peaceful. She died while having a cuddle...she died in my arms."

This was just a small vicious bit of spite from me. I wanted the mother to know that Mia was snuggled in arms that loved and adored her.

Not arms that abused.

She died with a face close to hers that kissed her and sang her lullabies.

Not a face screwed up with hatred and bitterness and anger.

The coroner decided to give a 'narrative judgement' on the cause of death and she concluded that;

Mia died as a result of Bronchial Pneumonia due to her general debility and immobility, which was as a result of brain damage caused by a non-accidental injury. Ethosuximide intoxication was present and this could have been as a result of a number of interconnecting factors; liver dysfunction and the interference of another drug with the metabolising of the Ethosuximide.

Ultimately, she died as a result of a non-accidental head injury, for without that, Mia would not have been on this medicinal regime.

As sad as it is, I was so glad to be exonerated of any wrong doing with regard to giving Mia her medication. The narrative judgement made it clear who had actually murdered Mia…her birth parents and not her foster parents.

Because Mia didn't die as a direct result of her head injury, the police were helpless in bringing anyone to real justice.

I live in the hope that the mother one day accepts her part in the death of an innocent child. Though doubt that will ever happen.

Mia's mother reclaimed her little body and, though she didn't want me to know when and where the service was held, I knew.

My baby was finally laid to rest.

Postscript

As with all foster carers we always hope for a 'Happy ever After' for the children that share our lives.

It is very sad when this doesn't happen for a variety of reasons, especially if the reason is that families don't want to adopt a child that has grown from a baby to a toddler or, as with Mia, because the baby doesn't have the chance to grow to a toddler because they have profound disabilities.

For us as a family the only real justice we had was the knowledge that, though the mother may have kept Mia in an urn somewhere in her house, Mia is now free and running with the angels...and the mother, following several more pregnancies was denied the opportunity of doing any damage to them as they were all removed at birth and placed for adoption straight away...let's hope they all get their Happy Ever After...

The Loss of Your Child
There's a pain beyond imagining
That's burning in your heart
For suddenly your whole world
Has been cruelly ripped apart
All words of consolation
Which are bound to come your way
Will probably seem empty
And of little use today
For when you ask for reasons
When you ask the question "Why?"
It makes no sense at all
That one so precious has to die
The only source of comfort
Is your memories, and the love
And they will shine forever
Like the brightest star above
A flame that burns eternally
So strong it lights the sky
And even through your darkest days
That flame will never die
So many people share your pain
We grieve with you as one
The gift of life gets taken back
But love goes on and on.

(Author unknown)

www.lizziescottbooks.com

Printed in Great Britain
by Amazon